RESEARCHING GENDER-BASED VIOLENCE

Researching Gender-Based Violence

Embodied and Intersectional Approaches

Edited by

April D. J. Petillo *and* Heather R. Hlavka

NEW YORK UNIVERSITY PRESS
New York

NEW YORK UNIVERSITY PRESS
New York
www.nyupress.org

Library of Congress Cataloging-in-Publication Data
Names: Petillo, April D. J., editor. | Hlavka, Heather R., editor.
Title: Researching gender-based violence : embodied and intersectional approaches / edited by April D.J. Petillo and Heather R. Hlavka.
Description: New York : New York University Press, [2022] | Includes bibliographical references and index.
Identifiers: LCCN 2021047242 | ISBN 9781479812189 (hardback ; alk. paper) | ISBN 9781479812202 (paperback ; alk. paper) | ISBN 9781479812226 (ebook) | ISBN 9781479812219 (ebook other)
Subjects: LCSH: Women—Violence against—Research—Methodology. | Abused women—Research—Methodology. | Women's studies—Methodology. | Feminist theory.
Classification: LCC HV6250.4.W65 R4589 2022 | DDC 362.88082—dc23/eng/20211005
LC record available at https://lccn.loc.gov/2021047242

CONTENTS

FOREWORD

JENNIFER R. WIES AND HILLARY J. HALDANE

What Remains

To study gender-based violence is to study humanity. It is impossible to explore or research any social or cultural topic and not encounter gender-based violence. Precisely because of its enveloping nature, gender-based violence is a well-studied topic across the social sciences, natural sciences, humanities, and fine arts. However, despite its ubiquity as a topic of study and a field of intervention, we sometimes no longer see it, the way it clings to us, the way we are shaped by it as we in turn reproduce it in miniature and across scale.

We are facing a crucible moment in academic research, in our studies of violence, and our very existence on this planet. The previous frameworks for how we have analyzed harm and human rights, prevention and power, and care and concern seem inadequate when faced with an epochal transformation of our political economy and social institutions. The authors herein capture this timeliness by synthesizing the corporal and the conceptual, to provide a new way of thinking from, with, and through our embodied entanglements and engagements. This book is one where you did not realize there was something new to say until you felt changed by the encounter.

April D. J. Petillo and Heather R. Hlavka have curated a noteworthy intervention that warmly embraces previous works and challenges us to take up new directions in gender-based violence studies, a field that feels at times like a worn and tired area of work. Yet this book is unique because it offers more than an intervention. It is a disruption, an eruption of anger, pain, pride, and hope. It compels us as readers to consider how wholly inadequate our fumblings have been heretofore and offers the unsettling we need to see the terrain with fresh eyes.

Humanizing Methodologies

This book situates the authors' experiences as researchers in a world that Dorothy Counts, Judith Brown, and Jacqueline Campbell did not live in when *To Have and to Hit* was first published. It is even a different world from the time *INCITE!* was written. Petillo and Hlavka draw from the elders while recognizing that the new generation of scholars see differently, think differently, and do differently. They put identity front and center. They embody the argument that the topic and the study is impossible to separate from the people who are doing it. Sarah Deer (Muscogee) in her 2015 book *The Beginning and End of Rape* writes, "There are different categories of knowledge. There is the kind of knowledge we gain from years of careful study, consulting as many experts as possible and analyzing the empirical data. Then there is the kind of knowledge we can from experiencing something; a visceral knowledge that can invoke the physical senses and the genius of memory. I find Athabascan scholar Dian Million's description of this as 'felt theory' particularly worthwhile because it honors and values the real, lived experiences of Native women as legitimate sources of knowledge. Both categories of knowledge are critical for addressing rape" (14). In Deer's use of "felt" knowledge, we see connections to the embodied and entangled methodologies that Petillo and Hlavka curate. The contributors go beyond a visceral reactive position that has often been divided into "firsthand experiences" with violence or "secondary trauma" and instead points to the layered and scaled ways that violence leaves a heavy touch for many, a lighter brush for a few. Petillo and Hlavka disrupt the ecological model to present instead a methodology that uses the warp and weft of our encounters with others, and with ourselves, that leaves one changed from listening to and learning from another's violence.

This book is born of an era that places the importance of identity at the forefront, by virtue of both the participants in our research and the people who are doing it. It is the latter set of voices that emerge radically, emotionally, and critically. The contributors challenge readers to interrogate the very nature of feminist methodology when it is embodied, entangled, and engaged with victims and survivors of gender-based violence. We are called to begin with Sherry Ortner's feminist assertion that we fundamentally use our own bodies as a "way of knowing" and then iteratively go further to acknowledge that the knowing is already influenced by the violence we study.

The book evokes a productive marriage between standpoint theory and interpretive labor. The recognition of the complexity of identity in conjunction with the work, the actual labor that is required to witness, see, hear, learn from, learn with. Thus, we are left with deeper questions: What becomes of feminist methods in this framing of our experiences as interconnected? How deeply does participation need to be felt? If we are embodied and entangled, what is observation—if not of ourselves as well as others?

Call to Action: What Next?

The call to action that this book demands is a humbling one: it is not only acceptable but is in fact necessary to change our minds, to critique our past confidence. If we are unwilling or unable to see the limits to what we believed to be true if only five years ago, five months ago, we are not engaging in felt, embodied, and entangled methodologies.

Today, we can hold sacred the potential that the world can one day be free of gender-based violence. Petillo and Hlavka's book represents a watershed moment in the political economy of academe: the legitimization of the theory and practice of gender-based violence research that not only recognizes but embraces the primacy of identity, lived experience as knowledge, and validates the expertise that comes from the aging process and the life cycle. It also represents how collaboration, collectivism, and, yes, engagement with coconspirators are the social bonds required for true cultural transformation. Capitalism's false promise of individual success and achievement has built a world of hate and harm. This is not a world we have to continue to accept. Rethinking our methodologies allows us to remake our realities.

REFERENCES

Counts, Dorothy A., Judith K. Brown, and Jacquelyn C. Campbell, eds. 1999. *To Have and to Hit: Cultural Perspectives on Wife Beating.* Urbana: University of Illinois Press.

Deer, Sarah. 2015. *The Beginning and End of Rape: Confronting Sexual Violence in Native America.* Minneapolis: University of Minnesota Press.

INCITE!, eds. 2006. *Color of Violence: The INCITE! Anthology.* Cambridge, MA: South End.

Ortner, Sherry B. 1995. "Resistance and the Problem of Ethnographic Refusal." *Comparative Studies in Society and History* 37 (1): 173–93.

Introduction

Recognition: Where Our Embodiment Entangled Us

APRIL D. J. PETILLO AND HEATHER R. HLAVKA

Women and scholars of color have gathered for decades to discuss how their lives and identities have impacted their approaches to investigating, documenting, analyzing, and theorizing about gender violence. This volume's community of contributors, and those who have added to our conversation about embodied methodologies over the past several years, are no exception. In large and small ways, this impulse to gather and discuss the violence laced through our lives has been a gift that has validated what we are otherwise told to ignore. Our culture and the academy tend to paint gender violence survivors and researchers as a collection of fragile, despondent figures that mostly mirror one another, tragically threaded together by trauma and sameness. Rather, our work reveals how violence reaches across many identities, intricately threading together vibrant communities even if others fail to recognize it. Working in academic and activist fields that often ignore scholarship on gender violence as "women's work" or, worse yet, "their/your work," our conversations between conference sessions, over text messaging, and in the occasional phone or zoom call, have anchored us and proven lifesaving for many.

The chapters that follow took shape in conversations between this book's coeditors and contributors, growing from conference panels, workshops, and roundtables to form this book. Despite our differences across multiple axes of identity, we could pinpoint how embodiment not only informed but enhanced our research projects. We shared our stories of how feminist researchers from varied disciplines, working in various sites, relied on the knowledge gained from living in their bodies to inform the techniques they used to identify, select, process, and analyze information on gender-based interpersonal violence. Doing so, we came to realize that we were not only embodying elements of our feminist gender violence work but also entangled in it. We were not alone. Open, public conversations at conferences were often replete with other gender violence scholars longing for more discussions on how to weave together the affective and intellectual in methodological practice and care ethics in gender violence work (Mulla and Hlavka 2011). While these conversations allowed for better insight and disciplinary understanding in the moment, there were still lingering questions. How could scholars harness the relationships, the material conditions, and intersubjective experiences to be publicly recognizable and remain respectful to what we have witnessed? How could we transgress the academy's disconnection and dislocation to transform gender violence research? What was it that simultaneously isolated us yet drew us together in these affective entanglements, and how can reflection, radical (sometimes brutal) honesty, and solidarity remedy the tangled web? Is "objective" *dis*entanglement even a worthwhile goal with this subject matter?

This book begins to answer some of those questions, gathering critical methodological reflections from people studying and living gender-based violence experiences across disciplines, fields, and positions. We start by asking ourselves where our identities intersect with and inform our sociocultural perspectives on gender-based violence, especially as writers who may embody the same tropes that entangle us and our disciplines. Those questions ground this volume, which argues for a more self-conscious and introspective methodological approach that prioritizes embodied, entangled knowledge instead of pretending that it neither exists nor provides valuable insight. This book rests on the far-reaching exploration of gender violence and forms of justice that applied scholars, practitioners, and activists work toward and against in their interventions. The authors have varied and vast herstories researching, writing, witnessing, and living the varied legacies of gender-based violence. While both senior and emerging scholars have contributed ideas shaping this final product, we have privileged emerging generations of gender violence scholars challenging the cognitive, "objective" researcher identity that is often weaponized throughout the academy. Our sister-friends, activists, and interlocutors have engaged us meaningfully, challenging us to rethink and unlearn, and have led the way toward feminist accountability in our fields. As a group, we do not fit the image imposed on us. Our commitment to include diverse experiences in this volume were both situated and shaped by contributors' capacities and constraints. Thus, this work is neither as complete nor diverse as we would like. We look forward to future companion collections that focus on areas unaddressed in this volume and privilege activist positionalities and geographies that we were unable to include here.

A Roadmap to This Collection and Its Use

This book is a blend of theory, experience, reflection, and empirical study steeped in the idea of unsettled witnessing, which Annie Fukushima (2016) frames as active refusal of the role of "passive observer." We expand on this concept to assert that feminist-identified gender violence research requires this kind of refusal of compartmentalized "academic comforts." Embracing such comforts only serve to ensure a judgmental distance that serves the academic institution instead of the pursuit of knowledge, the betterment of the social condition, or enhanced understanding of our shared humanity (Petillo 2020). Thus, organically and intentionally, the volume is embodied and entangled itself—a mix of critical methodological approaches and reflections in varied academic and narrative tones. We consider the benefits and complications of using feminist embodied methodology in gender violence research and the resulting representation and autonomy problems that are inseparable from social context and social justice. This volume challenges gender violence researchers, advocates, and activists to engage with critical introspection and build self-reflective and embodied methodologies. The book's contributors address these goals and open a broader dialogue on the following questions:

- What is the role and work of reflective methodology that recognizes (institutional) intersectional inequalities (rather than focusing on identity politics) in our research? How do we recognize and respond to the structures that maintain research violences?
- How is an embodied approach a new and/or adaptive form of feminist methodological praxis? What kinds of insights might this offer that are different from what was available before?

- What is the impact of engaging an embodied feminist methodology to gender-based violence? How are we affected as researchers, as knowers, and as producers of knowledge?
- What are the ethical considerations and the political challenges of embodied research and methodologies? What do we foresee as best and/or emerging practices in this kind of approach to gender-based violence? How can we reimagine our communities?

Turning our gaze inward, toward ourselves, is a means to appreciate how violence is a lived experience across multiple, intersecting bodies of oppressions, including our own. As a collective, the coeditors and contributors recognize the main challenges, navigate embodied research between researcher and interlocutor, and write "against the hierarchy" informed by insights from our resulting entanglements. *Researching Gender-Based Violence* includes ten chapters, divided into three parts, that cumulatively build toward reengaging our embodied imaginations.

Part 1: Naming: Intersectional Entanglements and Embodied Experiences

Part 1 begins with a brief history of the sociological and anthropological turn toward embodied knowledges, defining embodied methodology as a decidedly feminist approach to understanding the realities of gender violence. The three chapters that follow detail scholars' field experiences naming their entanglements in embodied methodologies and the impact of those entanglements on their work in those settings. This section is particularly helpful for understanding the basic concepts behind an embodied and entangled approach to research, as well as the epistemological and methodological links. Naming requires awareness and an understanding of how our social identities intersect and create different vulnerabilities and/or compliance demands. Part 1 begins to address the academy's colonizing practices on bodies, beings, and knowledge through this initial process of naming. The section also helps readers identify methodological practices and choices that rely on embodied knowledges in gender violence research and analysis and how it supports our work as coconspirators. This section will be particularly beneficial for anyone grappling with how to identify some of the ways researchers are both knowledge seekers and producers and to discuss the challenges of engaging this kind of research with feminist ideals of empowerment, equity, and intersectional parity.

Part 2: Being: Reflective Entanglements and (Academic) Violence by Another Name

The three chapters in this part delve deeper into how embodied methodology impacts *being* a researcher of gender violence. Recognizing how context is defined and understood through the body (embodiment) opens new data-collection areas and insights. Self-reflective attention to the context of being a human observer/witness with one's inner dialogue is central to this process. This section's contributors grapple with dominant discourses and compartmentalization, offering reflections on how listening to one's "inner vocabulary of actions" can help researchers filter troublesome issues (Petillo 2020). Topics discussed include managing the "messiness" of participant stories in tension with researcher training and disciplinary orientations. What we phrase "violence by another name" recognizes how participants' words, hesitations, and alternative standpoints get drowned out by dominant discourses, especially in the academy. This part also demonstrates how researchers' own trauma can inform structural violences inscribed on interlocutors. Both limit valuable interlocutor perspective on gender violence and perpetuate state-led and religiously sanctioned structural and interpersonal violences. Together, the contributors address work within familiar spaces and the tensions of shifting positionality as well as perspective. They interrogate the toll of institutional sexism and racism in both nonprofits and academic canons to generate concepts and ideas based on the ability to notice, shift, and be unsettled. This part will be particularly useful for both applied and academic researchers and students seeking ideas about how to navigate the complexities of gender violence research and to challenge the normalization of objectivity perpetuated at the expense of interlocutors and researchers alike.

Part 3: Witnessing: Entanglements That Humanize Our Methodologies

In part 3, contributors consider what an embodied approach means for reading and writing the multilayered landscapes of gender violence. The authors' primary focus includes the process of being embodied and entangled with our interlocutors and within our research sites, including the images and knowledges rendered through that work. Witnessing shifts our focus and ability from naming and being toward responding and cocreating. It is awareness of the mixes of vulnerability, agency, and power that comes from deep listening and engagement between bodies through verbal and nonverbal interactions. Two of these chapters specifically reflect on the work of "studying up" with elite populations and in oppressive systems that make decisions about the safety, protection, and freedoms of those who harm and those who have done harm. Together, the chapters viscerally bring the reader into the world of embodied methodology, connecting the complex gendered and racialized interplay between interpersonal and state violence. The authors reveal related and shared vulnerabilities in sensationalist spaces bent on dehumanization and exploitation through the spectacle of difference (Hartman 1997). This part is constructive for those who are navigating concerns about which tropes or common, repeated metaphorical or rhetorical ideas, motifs, clichés, or ideologies are used to render some voices silent and amplify others in gender violence research. Contributors describe methodologies of empowerment and healing through the body and describe processes of collaborative, intersectional, and team-based research approaches that focus on affective analyses. These innovative suggestions move the reader into the conclusion of the volume, where we settle ourselves within embodied imaginations.

This collection's conclusion offers insights into the original questions inspiring this book and considers the broad answers provided by the contributors. The purpose is to (re)imagine research as an interactive process shaped by the multilayered herstories and positionalities embodied in our work. We call for future interpersonal, gender violence research methodology with a firm grounding in the intersectional realities for individuals, communities, and researchers while recognizing that these three positions are hardly ever discrete. This closing chapter highlights what is to come of our work as we interrogate, share, and collaborate across fields, disciplines, and lived realities. In closing, we acknowledge that, when done well, our work requires introspection, contemplation, and time. Our work also requires both presence and practice engaging in innovative, inclusive, and affirming methodologies that simultaneously engage in and move beyond text and talk.

REFERENCES

Fukushima, Annie Isabel. 2016. "An American Haunting: Unsettling Witnessing in Transnational Migration, the Ghost Case, and Human Trafficking." *Feminist Formations* 28 (1): 146–65.

Hartman, Saidiya. 1997. *Scenes of Subjection: Terror, Slavery, and Self-Making in Nineteenth-Century America.* New York: Oxford University Press.

Mulla, Sameena, and Heather Hlavka. 2011. "Gendered Violence and the Ethics of Social Science Research." *Violence Against Women* 17 (12): 1509–20.

Petillo, April. 2020. "Unsettling Ourselves: Notes on Reflective Listening beyond Discomfort." *Feminist Anthropology* 1 (1): 14–23.

PART I

Naming

Intersectional Entanglements and Embodied Experiences

Frequently, the nudge to reconsider our methodologies only comes when we face a provocation. Perhaps the usual textbook research agendas and formulas never seemed to fit quite right with our interlocutors' lived realities. Perhaps we found ourselves triggered, sensing, and feeling the substantive differences between our experiences in the field, the academy, and in our lives as we struggled to disentangle them from disciplinary constraints that are more easily maintained when we do not meet our interlocutors face-to-face. To discuss how embodiment impacts our methodologies, we must first name how we recognize our own and others' embodied knowledge and our shifting ability to identify how we associate with social bodies and social identities. We must also recognize the centrality of our intersecting identities and its impact on doing research within institutional and social spaces that often valorize disembodiment of knowledge and social justice. Commonly, that is through the research entanglements in which we find ourselves.

How do you know that you are entangled? What is the moment of recognition?

Early in the conversations that sparked this volume, a group of us sat contemplating how to move forward from a wounding academic conference session. We held different academic positions, were of different ages, sexualities, ethnicities, races, family structures, and brought with us varied personal experiences of gender-based violence. The session began well, full of both devastating and inspirational revelations eloquently displayed in images, put into charts, and squeezed into succinct quotes on slides timed to the fifteen-minute interval. After the panel, we tried to hold onto the good feeling, reveling in new connections between our projects and inspiration where others' work or approaches challenged us to do better. The questions and comments offered additional challenges and thoughtfully encouraged participants to respond.

Then, the moment came, like it always does, when the great session quickly turns sour. An audience member stood, confident in his ingenuous entitlement, expecting an education on the basics of gender violence. With his one question, the air left the room. After a beat, we found ourselves fending off the usual queries that often come from those outside our field or, perhaps, from voyeuristic consumers of the research. These kinds of questions are often incessant and quickly tossed into the air: "Why do they stay if it isn't safe?" "Who wouldn't expect that kind of attention if they were in that area of town?" "How could women batter?" "Doesn't being a sex worker mean that you'd expect this kind of violence?" These questions land just as quickly as they rise to fill the air and time, like a gelatinous mass of words in the middle of the floor.

The mass threatened to spread. Panelists looked at each other, then at the moderator, who looked to allies in the audience. All of us, individually and collectively, instinctively know why these questions hit so hard. They demonstrate a lack of care for our interlocutors, weightier for the lack of compassion embedded in the academy that anchors the disregard. We also feel the direct impact—victim/survivor or not, frontline worker or not. It hits because we know, on multiple levels, the struggle of that lived life. Our knowledge is deeply embodied as we bear witness to and/or experience the struggles of our interlocutors, we are affected, and we affect. As we are prone to do, we defended our collective selves, lobbying well-researched responses in the direction of the gelatinous question mass—barely finishing before another of us piped up, on the ready to fill in. Despite the impromptu yet well-coordinated response and the exiting audience, the gelatinous question mass remained. The questions never fully disappeared. In this instance, we looked at each other and knew. Gathering on the sofas just beyond the room's entryway, one of us gave it words. "That makes me so damn angry, the kind of angry that makes me want to scream manically then smash rearview mirrors as I ride home from work on my bike, with shrill laughter trailing behind me." We did not say much more. We could not and did not need to. We had all been there. Recognition.

The focus of the panel was on violence prevention and the process of navigating the social and cultural conditions of living in violent relationships. This panelist's anger came from the deep-seated recognition of a combination of representations, requirements, and realities. Her anger stemmed from knowing that her argument (that we hold systems accountable for gender violence) was not the focus of intervention or social change. No matter how nuanced the analysis, she was always asked to explain anew, and convince anew, that the issue was not individual vulnerability or lack of agency. The issue was the institutional and structural violence allowing these conditions to continue. In moments like these, we are reminded of the artificial lines between researcher and participant, that the knowledge we produce has been shared, shaped, and interpreted by many of the same sociocultural harms and privileges. And in these realities and requirements, we cannot be shielded from knowing that our work can, and is, used to explain atrocities with empirical logic. This part of the book comes from these moments. Those moments fuel questions about how we shape our methodologies to consider the inseparability of sensate experience and the lived reality of power, compliance, resistance, and negotiation.

There has been forward movement and innovation in gender violence research practice and praxis. These insights have pushed our respective fields and disciplines to consider the often-inherent violence of research. Engaging in gender violence research requires attending to frictions like knowing what it feels like to be observed, judged, and analyzed according to standards that bear little resemblance to lived realities. Some problems appear, then reappear, haunting us in ill-fitting moments that are ill contained by our analytical categories. Those haunting moments center questions about how a methodology more responsive to (institutional) intersectional inequalities (instead of identity politics) might shift our research. That shift also changes how we recognize and respond to the academic structures that require our complicity in maintaining research violences.

From this place, we begin this part by providing context for understanding embodied methodology anew in and through gender violence research. In chapter 1, "Embodied and Entangled: Addressing the Methodological Challenges of Feminist Gender Violence Research," we provide a framework for thinking about an embodied methodology that relies on introspection to honor the feminist goals of examining and addressing power imbalances that are relational, structural, and institutional. We further map important concepts for understanding what it means to be embodied and entangled, as well as the benefits—and most importantly—the necessity, of its use in gender-based violence research. While acknowledging the groundbreaking feminist work that has paved the way, we reorient the academic gaze toward visceral knowledge (Deer 2015) steeped in everyday, lived experience and labors. We reflect on how an embodied methodological approach both pushes and pulls us to reconsider feminist methodology and praxis anew. In times of increasing fragmentation within the academy as well as dislocation and disembodiment encouraged throughout the world, we reach back toward each other for transformation and social change.

Brendane Tynes begins the process of "naming" in chapter 2, "'Sometimes There Just Ain't No Magic in This': Black Women at the Nexus of Gendered Violence and Erasure." Tynes considers intersectional truth-telling through a Black feminist ethnography that takes up ethics of care centered on Black women writing their lives rather than analyzing violent events in their lives. Tynes details a methodological praxis that accounts for where and how Black women's experiences as targets of both state and sexual violence have been erased, negated, or both through tropes about their innate ability to endure violence. Recognizing the historical and contemporary legacies of these tropes, Tynes explores ethnographic poetry as a medium for Black women to express the totality of their experiences, to connect with her interlocutors, and, together, to convey the complexities of sexual violence against Black women in an imperial, cis-heteropatriarchal state.

In chapter 3, "Interwoven Violence: Gender-Based Violence, Haunting, and Violence Research in Milpa Alta, Mexico City," Catherine Whittaker deconstructs the notion of violence as a purely "private" or "local" phenomenon. She demonstrates how global processes are implicated in violence against women, both on structural and intimate levels. Through ethnographic rural fieldwork, Whittaker considers how focusing on violence risks reducing people to their worst experience and thus masks how violence operates in their everyday lives. Doing so allows Whittaker to better see and *name* the experience of violence in the context of women's complex, often joyful, lives, rather than to reduce or flatten the complexity of their lives. Whittaker asks if it is possible to study violence against women without constructing women as victims in advance. Doing so, Whittaker questions the academic push to seek ways of framing others' lived lives to make sense, "rather than sense what was being made or undone in the moment of those encounters" (Whittaker, this volume; cf. Stewart 2017). The suggestion to affectively and intellectually attend to what is woven together or unraveled in the research process offers ways to "sidestep" research violence through (pre)categorization. This sidestep seems particularly important in considering how categorization "bestows the status of victimhood on some and refuses to recognize the victimhood of others," as Tynes also points out in her chapter in this volume.

Part 1 aptly culminates with Dawn Moore and Stephanie Hofeller's "The Language of Dissent: A Conversation between a Researcher and Participant-Turned-Collaborator on Studying Domestic Violence," which the authors self-assess as an unconventional "conversation that is not a conversation but is." Their chapter documents pivotal points in their collaborative work together as researchers/subjects, truth-tellers, and, eventually, friends. Moore and Hofeller address the deeply unequal structure of academic research that creates and reinforces power hierarchies in research on interpersonal violence. Writing about what is possible as "subjects" who have become collaborators and describing how those relationships unfold, Moore and Hofeller "write against the hierarchy." In the process, they address the subject experience of "observed and not listened to" and the researcher experience of ethically developing a relationship both aware of and beyond the power dynamic present in the participant/interlocutor and researcher roles.

Together, the chapters in part 1 name the laborious process of embodiment across unequal spaces and places, some of which we share with our interlocutors and some of which we do not. The authors reveal how emotions are analytic guides and how biographies can ground interpretations and shift vulnerabilities in research relationships, opening us all up to listening for alternative discourses, presented in part 2.

REFERENCES

Deer, Sarah. 2015. *The Beginning and End of Rape: Confronting Sexual Violence in Native America*. Minneapolis: University of Minnesota Press.

Stewart, Kathleen. 2017. "In the World That Affect Proposed." *Cultural Anthropology* 32 (2): 192–98.

1

Embodied and Entangled

Addressing the Methodological Challenges of Feminist Gender Violence Research

APRIL D. J. PETILLO AND HEATHER R. HLAVKA

Whether we admit it or not, researchers experience the world corporeally, with markers not entirely of our choosing. We embody the ways our bodies are identified or read externally, thereby becoming tangible social and cultural ideas, qualities, and feelings that we occasionally adjust. Regardless of how well we document reality, we do so with perceptions of the world that are at least partially shaped by others' interpretations of the meanings marked on our bodies. Though scientists are encouraged to seek impartial truths, with sensitive subject matter like interpersonal and gender-based violence, impartiality and objectivity may be neither worthwhile nor genuinely attainable goals. "The validity of the knowledge we create is the property not of a particular claim to truth, but of an open and critical discourse" (Sprague 2005, 197). We get better, more honest data in reciprocal research relationships based on shared personal and social experiences (Oakley 1981). Building trust and rapport in the communities we work in enhances solidarity with and advocacy for those whom we are committed to (Craven and Davis 2013). We inevitably do better, more thorough research when we work with communities that we are invested in, usually because they remind us of ourselves in some way (Schuller 2021). Their concerns and their freedom are ours. To paraphrase a colleague for this purpose, Why would you trust someone who could not understand how the structures that define your hell made your hell possible? Would you not prefer to work with someone who literally has had skin in the game or some other deep way of understanding your experiences?

More than a trick of alliteration, embodied entanglement describes the circular research experience of having insider perspective and lived experiences that can inform interpretation and research analysis. These perspectives and lived experiences are attained by moving through the world with identities that enhance our research projects and live outside of our positions as scholars/researchers. Lest we be persuaded otherwise, a passionate scholarship based in critical introspection creates the foundation for reciprocal relationships. As many sociology and anthropology scholars indicate, we often navigate toward our subject matter for very personal reasons (Deer 2016; Mills 1959), with feminist commitments to social change and social justice (Cook and Fonow 1986; Harding 1987; Oakley 2000). And while traditional research requires us to account for how our standpoint or positionality can make disciplinary insights harder to recognize (Petillo 2020a, 2020b; Navarro, Williams, and Ahmad 2013), intersectional identity informs scholarly insight in ways that are rarely recognized as beneficial. Gender-based violence research is anything but objective and is frequently the space where a researcher's intersectional identity can afford them additional insight into the mechanics of maneuvering victim/survivor realities, especially in relation to a system focused on carceral solutions (Richie 2012; Ritchie 2017). An embodied methodological approach anchors the researcher as a witness to sensitive, deeply personal areas of vulnerability while submerging them in their own exposure.

This book is grounded in anthropologists', sociologists', and sociolegal scholars' feminist thinking about interpersonal, gendered violence. Feminist anthropological genealogy dates to at least the late nineteenth century (Parezo 1993), while the theoretical school of feminist anthropology emerged in the 1970s (McGee and Warms 2004) with texts such as Peggy Golde's *Women in the Field* (1970), Michelle Rosaldo and Louise Lamphere's collection *Woman, Culture, and Society* (1974), and Rayna R. Reiter's volume *Toward an Anthropology of Women* (1975). Feminist sociology has a similar genealogical trajectory, from Dorothy Smith's (1974) sociological application and shaping of Sandra Harding's (1987) standpoint theory ultimately encouraging a rebel sociology that radically included the actualities of people's lives (Smith 1999). The theoretical work of women of color sociologists such as Patricia Hill Collins (2000a, 2000b) have pushed back, reshaped, and expanded our thinking on embodied knowledges, including Kimberlé Crenshaw's (1989) work encouraging us to consider the multiple ways that institutionally defined categories shape individual experiences of oppression. This volume stems from these thinkers and intellectual lineages while offering additional insight. This volume uniquely binds all these strands together, braiding a new rope to tether disciplinary and intersectional feminist inquiry.

Focusing deliberately on the work of gender violence research, this volume asks how methodology combines, as Harding (1987) notes, *epistemology* and *method*. Our theories of knowledge, or epistemology, are in reciprocal relationship with our choices about how we gather and interpret information. And while feminists have long argued for more creativity and introspection when it comes to research methodology, there are few specific articulations of how an embodied methodology can deeply situate knowledge as lived within sociopolitical contexts and consequences. We argue that an embodied approach to gender-based violence research takes up feminist intersectional theories and illustrates the concept of researchers witnessing and "listening through discomfort"—an embodied listening wherein self-reflection is deeply entangled (Petillo 2020b). In order to outline and demonstrate this approach, this chapter defines the major ideas and frames of reference that shape this practice and our thoughts on their use in gender violence research. After providing an explanation of embodied methodology, we discuss how "entanglement" and introspection provide additional insights.

Reconfiguring: The Embodied Turn in Social Science

All living is embodied. Enhanced, limited, and temporal, the physicality of our humanness and, therefore, the social and cultural meanings of that physicality are inescapable. And still, researchers carry on. Feminist theories have long negotiated the space between *corporality* and *sociality* that lies at the core of embodied theories, practices, and method. Yet the body has tended to lurk in the background of the social sciences. More than a physical, corporeal object, embodiment is the interplay between body and society, the site for the creation, mark, and maintenance of identity, oppression, violence, and harm. "Embodiment" refers to the role of the body in developing thoughts, qualities, ideas, and feelings. Feminist research assumes that the focus of study, or the subject, is a material/physical and embodied being that is interpretable or understandable in relation to the history, discourse, and cultural realties that create and contest it (Butler 1990, 1993; Collins 1998, 2000a, 2000b; Chaudhry 2000; Craven and Davis 2013; Davis 2013; Villenas 2000). Concepts once thought to be opposing, like the physical and the social, self or other, and natural or cultural, are treated as interactive (Grosz 1994). Thus, the corporeal is a site of social, political, cultural, and geographical inscription and production. The body is a cultural product instead of opposing culture, both a medium and a target of discrimination, discipline, oppression, and transgression (Bordo 1993; Moraga and Anzaldúa 2017).

Bodies become intelligible, legitimate, cast aside, or unthinkable through their ability to perform/meet social and cultural gender expectations (gender performativity). Thus, as Judith Butler (1990) argues, people make *gender trouble* through embodied acts and expressions that challenge binaries. Elizabeth Grosz (1994) details how experiences are grounded in bodies, as constructed cultural meanings inseparable from lived realities. Our bodies make our social actions and subjectivities visible to others as well, offering a site for others to understand us and, through that relational understanding, reflect or reveal us to ourselves. Susan Bordo (1993) and Mary Douglas (1966) theorize the body as a metaphor for culture, since meanings attributed to the body often represent larger social anxieties. Therefore, understanding embodiment is also understanding bodily boundaries and transgressions (Powell, Mulla and Hlavka, chapter 10 in this volume; Small, chapter 8 in this volume) and state violences (Mokhtar, chapter 7 in this volume), as well as shared narratives and poetry (Tynes, chapter 2 in this volume), sharing food (Whittaker, chapter 3 in this volume), and collective bodily transformation and healing (Brigden, chapter 9 in this volume). In "somatic societies," the body is a site of society and a signifier of social problems (Turner 1984, 1992). If "major political and personal problems are both problematized in the body and expressed through it" (Turner 1984, 1), then bodies are also sites of resistance, social change, and transformation.

The fundamental sociological reorientation toward the body (Turner 1984) relied on Michel Foucault's (1978) assertion that the body, as a site of surveillance, is (1) produced though power exercised to shape it and (2) generative in that it is an ongoing object of surveillance and discipline. Reading sociological theorists like Weber and Marx through this Foucauldian lens reshapes how we understand socially determined practices impacting bodies. Reshaping sociological concerns around producing ascetic and laboring bodies, as discussed by Weber in *The Protestant Ethic and the Spirit of Capitalism* ([1930] 1958) and Marx in *Writings of the Young Marx on Philosophy and Society* (1967), respectively, rewrites problems of social order (Parsons 1968), including perspectives of both the individual and body politic discussed as early as the seventeenth century (Hobbes 1651). Citing the body as the origin requires a phenomenological sociological approach, since embodiment is the consciousness and experience of the lived body. This corporeal sociology must also recognize that examining how society influences bodily existence, being, becoming, and reality (social ontology) requires also studying the corporeal production of bodies and how that production is interpreted (hermeneutic ontology).

Though steeped in cognitive traditions and disembodied approaches to social life, the social sciences have turned toward embodiment over the past several decades, tracking a variety of disciplines, fields, and methodologies. Despite a large and diverse body of scholarship on corporeality and embodiment (Shilling 2003; Turner 1984), work must expand the herstories of bodies, presence/absence of certain bodies, and the enfleshed experiences of embodied differences and inequalities (Ahmed 2017; Moraga and Anzaldúa 2017). Lived bodies are not reducible to a single discourse; they contain intersecting and interacting experiences, subjectivities, and forces. Researchers navigate their work enmeshed in embodied consciousness and experience, entangled in the cultural metaphor, frequently representing, on some level, what they investigate. This is no less true and, at times, potentially harrowing for gender violence researchers. Thus, an embodied, entangled framework incorporates the narrative body, situated in the self—and other—accounts of bodies, interwoven in the affective and intellectual and subsumed by institutional discourses.

The reflexive body, or *embodied reflexivity*, reveals how we turn our bodies into objects of our own bodily engagement through perceptions, emotions, body modifications, disciplining, comportment, and the like. It also calls attention to bodily disconnection or turning on/toward the body in moments of anguish, pain, trauma, or healing. Violence on/to the body, for example, impacts victims/survivors' physical and subjective integrity (Cahill 2001), regardless of whether it is in subtle, everyday interactions or structural or symbolic denials and inequities. When harmed, we interpret that embodied harm as ontology (making us) and epistemology (shaping our knowledge). Another disciplinary influence, the anthropological imagination, helps us to envision human connections and harms across cultural meanings that allow us to build as well as destroy what sustains us. Researchers who are critically trained to make meaning of the interconnected conditions and possibilities of human life across time can reflect on how gender violence is read through our own ideas, bodies, and kinship.

As researchers, we need our methodologies to consider the inseparability of sensate experience and the lived reality of power, resistance, and its negotiation. The living, knowing, reflexive body is an active subject and an expressive medium of behaviors, expressions, and emotions; it is cognitive and sensory. We cannot research without both.

An Embodied Methodological Praxis

Despite the substantial social science literature on bodies, affect, and embodiment, little work addresses how theory becomes methodological practice. How do we attend to fleshly narratives and affective bodies? What methods and practices are best suited to explorations of sensory experiences and expressions? The methodological process has always been a place where philosophy and theory mesh with research activity. It is also where praxis, that creative space where perspectives and ethics influence actual work practices, is born. Embodied methodology merges specific theories of feminist, sociological, and queer thinking into praxis that can enhance and expand philosophical approaches to gender-based, interpersonal violence research.

Feminist research emerged from concerns about traditional methodology's limited, if not wholly inadequate, insight into women's and other marginalized people's experiences within the human condition. Set in the dual role of reshaping academic institutions while operating within their confines, a constant across interdisciplinary and transdisciplinary feminist methodology is the push to create better knowledge about the experiences of people who are often ignored in traditional research. Feminist method works to demonstrate principles of respect for differing perspectives and attentiveness to power imbalances between researchers and their interlocutors. Instead of prioritizing a research method or strategy, feminist methodology allows the situation, context, and purpose to guide the choice of tools and techniques. One method may not be appropriate for every context and situation (Greaves et al. 1995). This is especially true when the goal is broadening the imaginary within which gender-based, interpersonal violence exists.

Queer theory or queered perspective generally requires one to call attention to the normalization processes that often go unnoted, including those that maintain rigid gender and sex binaries supporting hierarchal approaches to knowledge production. Emerging out of 1980s and 1990s academic activism during the AIDS crisis and decades of LGBTQ+ activism, this critical theory approach is particularly concerned with situating sexuality as a field of power, demonstrated by the published work of popular sociocultural thinkers and critics at that time, like Adrienne Rich ("Compulsory Heterosexuality and Lesbian Existence," 1980), Judith Butler (*Gender Trouble: Feminism and the Subversion of Identity*, 1990), Eve Kosofsky Sedgwick (*Epistemology of the Closet*, 1990), and Michael Warner (*Fear of a Queer Planet: Queer Politics and Social Theory*, 1993). Using Foucault's (1978) work on normalization and surveillance, queer theorists critique heteronormativity as it is related to a range of behaviors and categories in order to interrogate that which is labeled "deviant" or other. Concern lies in how binaries are perpetuated and create precarities for those who are labeled as deviant through cultural ideologies and practices. Relatedly, decolonial, feminist, and queer theorists have explained how social understandings have shaped our ideas about race, gender, sexuality, and (dis)ability. Rooted in social construction, such identities can act as culturally normalized expectations about behaviors, appearances, and how we relate to one another.

Intersectionality, most closely associated with the Combahee River Collective (2017) and Crenshaw (1989), is an analytical framework that challenges us to consider how we experience institutions from multiple experiences of oppressions (Collins and Bilge 2016). Intersectionality recognizes interlocking and entangled systems of oppression and privilege in structures and systems and through representation. For example, legal systems built to provide citizens protection, safety, and justice differentially respond to groups of people on the basis of their social and political locations. In many ways, the concept of intersectionality builds from Anna Julia Cooper's early assertion that one identity cannot be the primary factor in determining one's lived experience (*A Voice from the South: By a Black Woman of the South*, 1892). Intersectionality illuminates multiple forms of oppression and multiple membership to social categories and bodily markers like gender, race, sexuality, class, and (dis)ability. More than describing the individual experience of oppression or vulnerability, intersectionality focuses on systemic and institutional discrimination and erasure that function at the heart of structural violence. Here, that structure includes interpersonal, gender-based violence, as it is not sustained in a vacuum but in an ongoing and oppressive environment. The pervasiveness of gendered systems and normalization of gendered violence in relationships point to the urgency of this work and research. Experiences of gender violence are not the same in their manifestation, their symbolism, interactions, or structures, yet the approaches just outlined help harness the ability to see individual "troubles" as representative of larger systemic relationships (Mills 1959). Gender-based violence is structural when it interferes with rights to bodily integrity through law, policy, and political violations and practices. It is institutional in its marginalization and silencing of certain groups and peoples, and it is interpersonal in its application of social control through physical, emotional, symbolic, and psychological force and the threat thereof. With this understanding, embodied methodology is an extension of what many feminist researchers do already when they use their personal experiences of social institutions to better understand the inner workings, social sensitivities, and socially constructed frames to make sense of historical and contemporary social structures.

Embodied methodology requires reflection on how sensory and affective experiences impact research. That introspective space cultivates deeper self-knowledge and awareness. For researchers, that awareness includes how we are differently embodied and how experiences of gender, sexuality, race, ethnicity, class, and (dis)ability intersect with and within hierarchical positions and knowledges. This is especially significant in gender-based violence research, precisely because its endurance is entangled in our sociocultural identities. Research processes can alienate and invalidate victims/survivors (Das and Kleinman 1997), and we risk additional epistemic violence if victims/survivors do not recognize themselves in the research (Mulla 2008) because we have not "listened through discomfort" (Petillo 2020b) to get beyond our experience so that we can focus on theirs. Engaging and building a self-reflexive embodied methodology requires also grappling with how studies of gender-based violence can simultaneously perpetrate violence and oppression. We witness and write about violence and vulnerabilities as we (re)experience past and present violent and vulnerable contexts—including in the academy. Specifically, the embodied and entangled researcher must understand how to read their responses and position, or "vocabulary of actions," as a data source of the realities that are otherwise rendered invisible, inaudible, and unintelligible through an "objective" lens (Petillo 2020b). These otherwise-invisible data points threaten "research" as usual, shaking the glass barrier between researcher and subject even as they offer insight into trauma that is not and cannot always be spoken. Learning this vocabulary reveals a path for transdisciplinary listening across identities and intimacies, which is shared among people regularly experiencing structural, social, and cultural injustices.

When purposefully engaged, an embodied, entangled methodological practice allows for a multilayered view of the situation unhinged from murky objectivity. Instead, when researchers are attuned to their own vocabulary of actions, they are freed to honestly reflect on the observed recipient experience as well as on insight derived from the duality of researching and becoming part of the phenomena. The gender violence researcher is often dealing with life and death, thriving or surviving, and notions of what kinds of freedoms/constraints allow for a life "well lived," protecting both subject and self. An objective observer is not allowed to be present to what those feelings invoke. An embodied, entangled observer is invested and honors awareness and honesty with interlocutors. For instance, grappling with carceral approaches to violence interventions with an embodied, entangled approach is more complex when working with a victim/survivor whose face reminds you of a niece or nephew, child, partner, friend, or yourself. Thinking through feminist activist ethnographic ideals (Craven and Davis 2013), researchers who can harness their embodied, entangled potential are needed for the dynamic nature of the work.

REFERENCES

Ahmed, Sara. 2017. *Living a Feminist Life*. Durham, NC: Duke University Press.

Bordo, Susan. 1993. *Unbearable Weight: Feminism, Western Culture, and the Body*. Berkeley: University of California Press.

Butler, Judith. 1990. *Gender Trouble: Feminism and the Subversion of Identity*. New York: Routledge.

———. 1993. *Bodies that Matter: On the Discursive Limits of "Sex."* New York: Routledge.

Cahill, Ann. 2001. *Rethinking Rape*. Ithaca, NY: Cornell University Press.

Chaudhry, Lubna Nazir. 2000. "Researching 'My People,' Researching Myself: Fragments of a Reflexive Tale." In *Working the Ruins Feminist Poststructural Theory and Methods in Education*, edited by Elizabeth St. Pierre and Wanda S. Pillow, 96–113. New York: Routledge.

Collins, Patricia Hill. 1998. *Fighting Words: Black Women and the Search for Justice*. Minneapolis: University of Minnesota Press.

———. 2000a. *Black Feminist Thought: Knowledge, Consciousness, and the Politics of Empowerment*. 2nd ed. New York: Routledge.

———. 2000b. "What's Going On? Black Feminist Thought and the Politics of Postmodernism." In *Working the Ruins Feminist Poststructural Theory and Methods in Education*, edited by Elizabeth St. Pierre and Wanda S. Pillow, 41–73. New York: Routledge.

Collins, Patricia Hill, and Sirma Bilge. 2016. *Intersectionality*. Cambridge, UK: Polity.

Combahee River Collective. 2017. "The Combahee River Collective Statement." In *How We Get Free: Black Feminism and The Combahee River Collective*, edited by Keeanga-Yamahtta Taylor, 5–14. Chicago: Haymarket Books.

Cook, Judith, and Mary Fonow. 1986. "Knowledge and Women's Interests: Issues of Epistemology and Methodology in Feminist Sociological Research." *Sociological Inquiry* 56:2–29.

Cooper, Anna Julia. 1892. *A Voice from the South: By a Black Woman of the South*. Chapel Hill: University of North Carolina Press.

Craven, Christa, and Dána-Ain Davis. 2013. *Feminist Activist Ethnography Counterpoints to Neoliberalism in North America*. Lanham, MD: Lexington Books.

Crenshaw, Kimberlé. 1989. "Demarginalizing the Intersection of Race and Sex: A Black Feminist Critique of Antidiscrimination Doctrine, Feminist Theory and Antiracist Politics." *University of Chicago Legal Forum* 1989:139–67.

Das, Veena, and A. Kleinman. 1997. Introduction to *Violence and Subjectivity*, edited by V. Das, A. Kleinman, M. Ramphele, and P. Reynolds, 1–17. Berkeley: University of California Press.

Davis, Dána-Ain. 2013. "Border Crossings: Intimacy and Feminist Activist Ethnography in the Age of Neoliberalism." In *Feminist Activist Ethnography: Counterpoints to Neoliberalism in North America*, edited by Christa Craven and Dána-Ain Davis, 23–38. Lanham, MD: Lexington Books.

Davis, Dana-Ain, and Christa Craven. 2016. *Feminist Ethnography: Thinking through Methodologies, Challenges, and Possibilities*. Lanham, MD: Rowman and Littlefield.

Deer, Sarah. 2016. *The Beginning and End of Rape: Confronting Sexual Violence in Native America*. Minneapolis: University of Minnesota Press.

Douglas, Mary. 1966. *Purity and Danger: An Analysis of Concepts of Pollution and Taboo*. London: Routledge and Kegan Paul.

Foucault, Michel. 1978. *The History of Sexuality, Part 1*. New York: Pantheon Books.

Golde, Peggy. 1970. *Women in the Field: Anthropological Experiences*. Berkeley: University of California Press.

Greaves, Lorraine, Alison Wylie, Cheryl Champagne, Louise Karch, Ruth Lapp, Julie Lee, and Bina Osthoff. 1995. "Women and Violence: Feminist Practice and Quantitative Method." In *Changing Methods: Feminists Transforming Practice*, edited by Sandra Burt and Lorraine Code, 301–26. Toronto: Broadview.

Grosz, Elizabeth. 1994. *Volatile Bodies: Toward a Corporeal Feminism*. Bloomington: Indiana University Press.

Haraway, Donna. 1988. "Situated Knowledges: The Science Question in Feminism and the Privilege of Partial Perspective." *Feminist Studies* 14 (3): 575–99.

Harding, Sandra, ed. 1987. *Feminism and Methodology*. Bloomington: Indiana University Press.

Hobbes, Thomas. 1651. *Leviathan; or, The Matter, Forme and Power of a Commonwealth Ecclesiasticall and Civil*.

Marx, Karl. 1967. *Writings of the Young Marx on Philosophy and Society*. Edited and translated by Loyd David Easton and Kurt H. Guddat. Garden City, NY: Doubleday.

McGee, Jon, and Richard Warms. 2004. *Anthropological Theory: An Introductory History*. New York: McGraw-Hill.

Mills, C. Wright. 1959. *The Sociological Imagination*. New York: Oxford University Press.

Moraga, Cherríe, and Gloria Anzaldúa, eds. 2017. *This Bridge Called My Back: Writings by Radical Women of Color*. 4th ed. Albany: SUNY Press.

Mulla, Sameena. 2008. "There Is No Place like Home: The Body as the Scene of the Crime in Sexual Assault Intervention." *Home Cultures* 5 (3): 301–25.

Navarro, Tami, Bianca Williams, and Attiya Ahmad. 2013. "Sitting at the Kitchen Table: Fieldnotes from Women of Color in Anthropology." *Cultural Anthropology* 28 (3): 443–63.

Oakley, Ann. 1981. "Interviewing Women: A Contradiction in Terms." In *Doing Feminist Research*, edited by Helen Roberts, 30–61. London: Routledge and Kegan Paul.

———. 2000. *Experiments in Knowing: Gender and Method in the Social Sciences*. Cambridge, UK: Polity.

Parezo, Nancy. 1993. *Hidden Scholars: Women Anthropologists and the Native American Southwest*. Albuquerque: University of New Mexico Press.

Parsons, Talcott. 1968. *The Structure of Social Action: A Study in Social Theory with Special Reference to a Group of Recent European Writers*. New York: Free Press.

Petillo, April. 2020a. "Sketching Arrivantcy: Self-Naming toward Decolonized Solidarity across Indigenous and Black Divides." *Frontiers* 41 (2): 192–215.

———. 2020b. "Unsettling Ourselves: Notes on Reflective Listening beyond Discomfort." *Feminist Anthropology* 1 (1): 14–23.

Reiter, Rayna. 1975. *Toward an Anthropology of Women*. New York: Monthly Review Press.

Rich, Adrienne. 1980. "Compulsory Heterosexuality and Lesbian Existence." *Signs: Journal of women in Culture and Society* 5 (4): 631–60.

Richie, Beth. 2012. *Arrested Justice: Black Women, Violence, and America's Prison Nation*. New York: New York University Press.

Ritchie, Andrea. 2017. *Invisible No More: Police Violence against Black Women and Women of Color*. Boston: Beacon.

Rosaldo, Michelle Zimbalist, and Louise Lamphere. 1974. *Woman, Culture, and Society*. Stanford, CA: Stanford University Press.

Schuller, Mark. 2021. *Humanity's Last Stand: Confronting Global Catastrophe*. New Brunswick, NJ: Rutgers University Press.

Sedgwick, Eve Kosofsky. 1990. *Epistemology of the Closet*. Berkeley: University of California Press.

Shilling, Chris. 2003. *The Body and Social Theory*. London: Sage.

Smith, Dorothy. 1974. "Women's Perspective as a Radical Critique of Sociology." *Sociological Inquiry* 44 (1): 7–13.

———. 1999. *Writing the Social: Critique, Theory, and Investigations*. Toronto: University of Toronto Press.

Sprague, Joey. 2005. *Feminist Methodologies for Critical Researchers: Bridging Differences*. Lanham, MD: Rowman and Littlefield.

Turner, Bryan. 1984. *The Body and Society: Explorations in Social Theory*. New York: Blackwell.

———. 1992. "Weber, Giddens and Modernity." *Theory, Culture & Society* 9 (2): 141–46.

Villenas, Sofia. 2000. "This Ethnography Called My Back: Writings of the Exotic Gaze, 'Othering' Latina, and Recuperating Xicanisma." In *Working the Ruins: Feminist Poststructural Theory and Methods in Education*, edited by Elizabeth St. Pierre and Wanda S. Pillow, 74–95. New York: Routledge.

Warner, Michael. 1993. *Fear of a Queer Planet: Queer Politics and Social Theory*. Minneapolis: University of Minnesota Press.

Weber, Max. (1930) 1958. *The Protestant Ethic and the Spirit of Capitalism*. New York: Scribner.

2

"Sometimes There Just Ain't No Magic in This"

Black Women at the Nexus of Gendered Violence and Erasure

BRENDANE TYNES

"I can't die. I won't. Even when they kill us, we continue to live." The Balti-morean poet and artist Harmony began the memorial service by pouring water in the large fern in the corner.[1] "I will pour for each ancestor, each victim of violence. Each one of us will lift one up and invite her into the room." It was late July 2018 when poets, artists, and activists gathered in the common space that we dedicated to the memory of Black women and girls who had died due to interpersonal and state-sanctioned violence. Almost everyone in the room, when I arrived, identified as a woman or as a gender-nonconforming person. There were very few cisgender men present. This was similar to any other activist space I had been in, espe-cially those dedicated to Black women and girls.

After Harmony and another poet performed, the floor was opened for the attendees to offer elegies of their own. I performed a poem:

> I am the legacy of centuries old rape,
> culminating on April 15, 1987
> no June 1993
> no June 3, 2010
> no now . . .
> it seems as if my womanhood has become synonymous
> with sexual assault and battery
> my last name is abuse
> I inherited it from my mother
> who inherited it from her mother who
> witnessed it at the hands of her father—
> but he was not the beginning of this generational curse.

my mother often tells the story of the men who threatened her life
when she decided to terminate relationships
the consequences of ending their ownership were the same of a
    blood covenant to their abuse-loving god—
dumb bitch
a fist
I don't let go easily—
she toted a tiny gun with a diamond handle after she left my brother's
    father
because he looked at my little sister a little too long;
he admired her a little too much.
perhaps my mother could sniff the pedophilic demon on him
the scent of burning asphalt and brimstone pounding her nostrils
she remembers the morning she woke up engulfed in flames
she ran because she had always loved us more than she loved
    herself
and though she had never known a love that didn't hurt,
she dreamed that we would never know a love that did.

when I was sixteen, I learned how many breaths it takes to subdue
    one's intuition.
I took one too many when I followed him,
quieted my nerves,
the nagging at the base of my throat
he did not ask me any questions
just took what he thought was his
I escaped with what was left of me:
my breath, my skin but no words
that night I told my uncle, grandma, mother, and pastor
my uncle told me never to tell a soul
that boy simply misunderstood
no need to ruin his life when I could live with what remained

my paternal grandmother died when my father was fifteen.
my grandfather poisoned her
his love demanded that she want no other man

fast forward and I am twenty-one
and love's hands have locked around my throat
no breath to quiet my intuition so
I remember the feeling of loss
I/we have been here before

Shortly after my reading, a Black man named Michael entered the room with a white woman. They had been talking together in the room next to the healing space during most of the event, so their sudden appearance and interest in the event was noted. He raised his hand and asked to speak. "I don't know how I can honor Black women when my mother was not good to me. My father was never around, but she really caused me pain. I find it hard to be in a space that honors Black women when I feel the way I do." Instead of asking Michael to leave the space dedicated to honoring Black women and girls, the Black women activists began to empathize with him. Some shared stories of how they felt abandoned and betrayed by their fathers. The space dedicated to harmed and deceased Black women and girls transformed into a space to nurture this hurt Black man, who discounted the value that Black women brought to his life. His mother, who provided for him, was less valuable than his absent father. His grandmother, who had done the majority of the caretaking for him while his mother worked, was not even seen as a Black woman worth honoring. His feelings of hurt and neglect took priority over the memorialization of Black women and girls. Their vulnerability, evidenced by their deaths, was erased to create a space of comfort for him.

Michael's inability to recognize Black women's structural vulnerability as separate from his own troubled relationship to his mother and his feelings about her is a by-product of the systemic issue of erasure and negation of state-sanctioned and gendered violence against Black women. Calls to "fight for the souls of Black girls" (Green, Walker, and Shapiro 2020) or to "protect Black women" (Stallion 2020) have garnered recent national attention to a centuries-old problem. Movements like Kimberlé Crenshaw's #SayHerName and Tarana Burke's #MeToo address the erasure of violent experiences of Black women and girls; yet the erasure of their violability persists through the societal focus on

Black male vulnerability. The erasure and negation of Black women's violent experiences uplifts Black men as hypervulnerable victims of state violence and white women as the primary victims of sexual violence, erasing the nuanced ways that patriarchy, sexism, and anti-Blackness intersect in Black women's and girls' lives.

The sociohistorical construction of Black womanhood includes controlling images (Collins 2000) that depict them as perpetually sexual (Jezebel), perpetually motherly (Mammy), and/or perpetually angry (Sapphire). Through these controlling images, gendered violence against Black women is justified as a corrective for Sapphire's angry, bitter behavior, and Jezebel's overtly sexual nature "invites" violence. In the case of the Mammy, who is viewed as an asexual mother figure, violation is impossible. These archetypes make Black women and girls unthinkable victims of violence even as they organize and lead political movements against anti-Black and gendered violence. Even still, Black women's violent experiences outside of these images are rendered illegible, except through certain terms that remake their violations as evidence of Black men's unrealized patriarchal power or as testaments to Black women's ability to endure violence with supernatural strength. Here, I discuss the ways that Black women victim-survivors of interpersonal and state-sanctioned violence combat the erasure of their experiences through poetry.[2] I begin by briefly outlining the sociohistorical conditions that undergird the epistemic violence of the erasure of Black women's experiences. Then I argue that Black feminist ethnography must take up an ethics of care that rests in the ontological reality of Blackness and Black womanhood—a reality that excludes Black women from the normative definitions of "victim" that permeate research about gendered violence. Finally, I articulate a Black feminist practice of ethnographic poetry that highlights how Black women create the terms through which their experiences become legible.

A Herstorical Grounding

Black women experience a structural vulnerability, created through the racial-sexual violence of capture and enslavement that limited definitions of humanity and "true" womanhood to those who could seek legal redress for the violation of their bodies (Battle 2016; Hartman

1997; James 2013; Freedman 2013). Chattel slavery instituted a pervasive legal code that allowed for the violation of Black bodies writ large while rendering those bodies nonhuman. The law also reinforced the sexual exploitation of enslaved women in two ways: the child produced from rape was a slave, and the rape of an enslaved woman was not a crime (Roberts 1999). Legal cases cemented that enslaved people were not subjected to common law, only to the slave codes (statutory law), *but the rape of enslaved women was not recognized by either* (Hartman 1997). The prosecution of rape against Black enslaved women was impossible—constituting them as an unprotected yet highly vulnerable class of people.

In order to justify the enslavement of Black women, stereotypes about their strength, endurance, and animal-like qualities proliferated. The images of white women, depicted as fragile, chaste, and constantly in need of protection, contrasted with the images of Black women, cementing racial and gender-based hierarchies in society. There are misconceptions about when, where, and how Black women experience racialized gendered violence, often framed as "private" forms, such as rape, sexual assault, and/or intimate partner violence, versus "public" forms of violence, such as murder or lynching. The characterizations of "private" and "public" forms of violence erase Black women as victims of lynching and police violence *and* erase sexual violence as a form of police violence and state-sanctioned terror (Cole and Guy-Sheftall 2003; Spillers 1987). This vulnerability and erasure, the "materialized scene of unprotected female flesh," as Hortense Spillers names it (1987, 68), draws our attention to the particular condition of the Black enslaved woman and her descendants who continually reach but never fully grasp the patriarchal protection conferred on the female gender and who perpetually feel the distorting power of racialization. Put differently, Black women are denied the protections of white femininity (Davies 1994) that view sexual violence as a disruption to bodily integrity and a violation of (wo)manhood. Black women's bodies are not viewed as bodies that require protection or safety, and this allows for the violation of their bodies to go unnoticed and unaddressed or, even worse, to be *justified*.

Though Black men, women, and children are all affected by state-sanctioned violence, there is greater focus on the violence that Black men and boys experience (Ritchie 2017; Richie 2012; Crenshaw et al.

2016; Lindsey 2015; Garza 2014). The proliferation of images of dead Black male bodies not only shows state terror but also reinscribes patriarchal norms through the absence of images of Black women, girls, and gender-variant people, who also die from state-sanctioned violence. By naming Black cisgender men as the typical victims of police violence, Black women and girls are relegated to caretaking roles through maternal care work and leadership in racial justice movements.

Positioning Black women and girls as mothers of Black-led movements obscures the multiple vulnerabilities they experience at the hands of the police—where their racialized and sexualized vulnerabilities can be especially apparent. In September 2014, Daniel Holtzclaw, an Oklahoma City police officer, was indicted for charges of rape and sexual assault of at least thirteen Black women and girls. His pattern of sexual violence was discovered when he stopped grandmother Jannie Ligons while she was driving through her neighborhood. After patting her down, he made her sit in the backseat of his police car. He forced her to expose her breasts and her genitals, and he coerced her into performing oral sex on him. In her report to Democracy Now, Ligons described her fear and her later determination to seek justice. After Holtzclaw left her, she reported his violation at the police station. Shortly after, thirteen women came forward. Holtzclaw, like many police officers who commit acts of sexual violence, routinely targeted vulnerable women: teenagers, drug addicts, and sex workers. During his trial, Holtzclaw's defense mainly relied on racist tropes about Black women's behavior. He labeled his victims as "untrustworthy, inconsistent, high, and women with 'an agenda' based on their past criminal histories" (Ritchie 2017, 107). He implicitly leaned on centuries-old logic about the sexual virility and availability of Black women, especially the controlling Jezebel trope (Collins 2000; Hartman 1997; Feimster 2009; Harris-Perry 2011; Richie 2012). Thankfully, his defense failed, and he was convicted to 263 years in prison for his crimes.

Police sexual violence against Black women has always been a major part of state violence, yet it is often disregarded in conversations about police violence (Crenshaw 2012; Richie 2012; Ritchie 2017). When society chooses to measure the injustices of police violence through the violence enacted on the bodies of men, violence against women and girls is rendered invisible and thus becomes normalized. Narrowing the definition of what constitutes "police brutality" to the killing of a Black male body limits the ability to create a movement that truly changes the conditions of Black life (Tynes 2020).[3] State-sanctioned violence against Black women's and girls' bodies, and the invisibilization of that violence, upholds a racialized and gendered state of oppression that eliminates their ability to redress violence against them. They remain relegated to being participants in the movement to save Black men and boys. To remedy this, Treva Lindsey (2015) argues for an expansion of the understanding of the violability of the Black body through a "herstorical" approach that centers the experiences of Black women and Black gender-nonconforming, trans, and queer people. A herstorical approach to the study of state and sexual violence brings the stories of all Black people to light, not just those who fit white-supremacist, patriarchal, and heteronormative definitions of victim-survivors.

What's "Care" Got to Do with It? Black Feminist Approaches to Writing Violence against Black Women

the iterative nature of anti-black violence. the *ditto ditto*, the
excavation, the resettlement, the call to remember who your
people were, the call to forget what he/they/we did to you,
the inability to forget. the memory settled in your bones,
buried so it can't bring forth any fruit, you hold it here, inside, water it with salty tears like your momma and your
grandmother and your great grandmother who died before
she could see anything grow
—selection from author's untitled poem

Ethnography, as an anthropological practice, has roots entrenched in colonial violence. We witness this in traditional ethnographies that painted caricatures of the lives of African "exotic peoples" and relegated their bodies and daily practices to nonhuman in order to subjugate them. As ethnographers, we must be conscious of the ways that we re-present violence in our work. Writing about gendered violence using traditional methods developed by elite white men can lead to the reproduction of racist and sexist accounts of our interlocutors' lived experiences. As anthropologists, we must resist projects of "translation" that rely on pornographic snapshots of violence, written to prove objectivity, to show command of scientific knowledge, and to exotify the Other. These pornographic snapshots comprise elements of the epistemic violence that reinforces and simultaneously negates the vulnerability of certain populations (Mulla and Hlavka 2011). Sameena Mulla and Heather Hlavka draw on Gayatri Spivak's definition of "epistemic violence" to define it as "a subaltern defined by Western epistemology that defines and delimits the subaltern's 'voice' in a way that does not encapsulate the subaltern's subject position as viewed from the subaltern's perspective" (1513). Epistemic violence occurs when ethnographies do not represent a subject's experiences outside of paradigmatic Western epistemic categories and understandings.

One way that epistemic violence can be remedied is through an interdisciplinary practice of care ethics (Mulla and Hlavka 2011). Care is a mutually constitutive relationship between the ethnographer and the research subject, one that holds the ethnographer of sexual violence accountable to the victim. Care has sometimes been demonstrated in ethnographies about interpersonal violence as the "move away from analyses of the event of violence itself—[since the event is] an epistemic object that does not easily lend itself to analysis or to generalizable findings" (Mulla and Hlavka 2011, 1515). The current conundrum for many ethnographers has been writing and working within institutional structures that use Western epistemic categories to authenticate suffering, namely, legal and medical apparatuses (cf. Mulla 2008, 2014). These legal and medical apparatuses, such as rape kits, forensic exams, courtroom testimonies, and police investigations, often exact additional violence on victims of interpersonal violence as well. The feminist ethics of care moves the object of observation from the vulnerable, violated body to institutions that often perpetuate and compound the harm that the ethnographer aims not to reproduce. Studies that aim to decenter the body as an attempt to show care for their subjects can demystify the institutional violence that dictates who is the vulnerable victim. The ethos of care implies some kind of protection for the victim—defined intersubjectively among the vulnerable person herself, the researcher, and medical, legal, and social institutions.

What happens when the person violated does not fit into normative definitions of victimhood? Particularly, what happens if this person is a Black woman or girl? Care takes on a different register when writing about Black women's and girls' violent experiences because of their particular social positionality in the United States. In order to sustain the contemporary social fabric, the Black woman must be malleable yet fixed at the bottom within the prescribed "American grammar," the symbolic order that calls for both the symbolic and material deaths of Black people (Spillers 1987). Her flesh—which Spillers names as "a praxis and a theory, a text for living and dying, a method for reading both through their diverse mediations" (1987, 68)—is imbued with multiple, mythical meanings, which when read uncritically, reinscribe anti-Black, sexist devaluations of her body and her labor. Interrogating how we write Black women's and girls' bodies must tend to two problems at once: the hypervisibility of the violence against them, circulated and recirculated through media and institutions, and then the invisibility of violence against them (Romero 2000), subsumed under the depictions of the "endangered" Black man, the "fragile" white female sexual assault victim, and the "strong" Black woman. The malleability of the Black woman, which molds her existence as *always already* vulnerable to violence yet inviolable breaks apart normative forms of care, even those that can be written as feminist. We must recognize that the violation of Black women's bodies—and the inability to redress violence against them—is central to the construction of gender, womanhood, and victim. To answer Mulla and Hlavka's call to "consider the intersubjective construction of the category 'victim'" (2011, 1518), we must attend to Black women's experiences that have been epistemologically written as illegible to this categorization. Victimhood implies a sense of humanity, a recognition of vulnerability (Vargas and James 2013). How do we restore recognition of the possibility of vulnerability that is consistently denied to the Black female subject?

In order to conceptualize a Black feminist ethics of care that tends to the recognition of Black women's lived experiences, I draw on a variety of methods in anthropology, Black studies, and critical literary theory. I have found that it is not enough to "care" for Black women and girls through writing about their interactions with violent institutions. It is not enough to issue calls to "protect" them inside and outside of ethnographic writing without tending to the misrecognition of their vulnerability. A Black feminist ethics of care requires a shift in our normative definitions of the feminized practice of "caring" for each other, often grounded in anti-Black, patriarchal understandings of whose bodies necessitate protection. In writing about Black women, care must have a deeply political character that is tied to the pursuit of liberation. I see this care work as a form of "wake work," a practice defined by Christina Sharpe (2016) that recognizes anti-Black violence and Black death as normative and productive in an effort to disrupt the dysgraphic representations of Blackness. In wake work, we pay special attention to the ways that the rupture of slavery reemerges in the present, lived conditions of Black people and in conditions of Black death and violation. Blackness has an anagrammatical nature: fracturing the meaning of words like "woman," "human," and "child" to describe the subjugated positions of those who can be described as a *Black* woman, *Black* person, or *Black* child. Caring for the *Black* victim-survivor, then, takes on a new meaning, necessitating that we transform care from an affective state and ethical stance to a political stance evidenced through how we invite our interlocutors' experiences to the page.

The care required for wake work, for political freedom, for redress requires a certain type of remembering that is historically grounded and resists colonial logics of objectivity. Care for a Black victim-survivor might take different forms in the world: giving one what they need to survive in this anti-Black world, giving one the tools to escape, or the refusal to let a loved one be misremembered after death and/or violation. Care is not simply displacing bodily violations onto institutions as a means to recuperate a sense of bodily integrity or "humanity" but a recognition of how those systems operate in, through, and outside of violated bodies. The critical Black feminist anthropologist, then, is tasked with the project of care through ethnographic and Black feminist epistemological methods that elucidate the concrete ways in which power has prescribed and inscribed meaning onto Black women's and girls' bodies. The reading of Black women's lives, of the lived conditions of their flesh in the American grammar, requires one to consider how they *actually* live, and this can be done uniquely through ethnographic poetry.

The Power of Black Feminist Ethnography and Poetry

Sometimes there just ain't no magic in this . . .
—Mecca, Baltimorean poet and activist

In this section, I describe the Black feminist ethnographic practice of poetry that I employ with my interlocutors. I aim not to reproduce epistemic violence of centering their words as pilfered snippets that bolster a theoretical argument or positioning them as objects of violence who merely write to cope.

For artists like Mecca, whose words have formed the first part of this chapter's title, the future for Black women and girls would be one that would allow them to be ordinary, where they would not have to exist as magical or superhuman figures. Mecca centers much of her poetry on the "ordinary" experiences of Black female life in Baltimore. During the memorial service described at the beginning of this chapter, she performed several pieces that centered her own experience living with violence and mental health issues. Through her poem "Things to Unlearn," Mecca described her desire to live in a world where she can wallow in her depression without the guilt of not being "strong enough" to lead new movements, nor would she have to be "strong enough" to mourn the lives of Black women and girls killed too soon. She pushed everyone in attendance to question the utility of the anti-Black stereotype of Black women's innate ability to endure, formerly recognized as the "Superwoman Syndrome" (Wallace [1979] 2015) and often misnamed "Black Girl Magic." By unlearning the epistemic violence of anti-Black misogyny, she could embrace the ordinary and the complex. She could embrace her vulnerability.

There is no magic formula for living as a Black woman at the intersection of multiple forms of oppression, yet the silences around our experiences still render them a mystery. The depersonalization of racism, which Audre Lorde says creates "a distortion of vision" in which "Black women have on one hand always been highly visible, and so, on the other hand, have been rendered invisible" (1984, 42), forms the ground on which Black women create the terms by which their violation is recognized. My interlocutors, like many other Black women, realize that the world—even with its best, most antiracist intentions—will marginalize, misrecognize, spectacularize, and erase their violent experiences, and yet they speak and write anyway. Black feminist ethnography provides an opportunity for Black women's stories to become centered through practices that are "self-consciously fashioned as an act of knowledge production and [see themselves] as a form of cultural mediation between the world of Black scholars and the entire Western intellectual tradition, between Black anthropologists and the rest of the discipline, and between Black and white feminists" (McClaurin 2001, 2). The close-read, "herstorical" approach to the study of the lives of Black women brings to bear the complexities of life at the intersections of many forms of oppression that upend the white feminist notion that some universal form of patriarchy is the root of evil in all women's lives. My interlocutors and I often find poetry to be a useful medium to convey these complexities.

Using poetry as a tool to convey the emotions and practices of daily life requires an expert use of language and a vulnerability that is not typically present (or welcomed) in scholarly texts. Poetry emerges out of an ancient, deep, dark place of power, as a "revelatory distillation of experience" that transforms the nameless into the named (Lorde 1984). The deep, dark place of power is a space for the critical reflection, the grappling of language, and at times, the incommunicability of Black women's and girls' experiences with violence: upending the epistemic violence that claims that Black women are not apt narrators of our own experience. Through poetry, Black women tell in our own words how we experience life at the intersection. This Black feminist approach to writing ethnographic poetry grounds itself in Black women's lived experiences without the pornotroping display of violence and violation (Spillers 1987; Hartman 1997), resisting the societal myths that Blackness equals trauma and that Black women handle that trauma especially well. When written by the Black feminist ethnographer, poetry breaks apart the "ethnographic gaze" by tightening the gap between her experiences and the experiences of her interlocutors. This art form conveys the complexity of emotion in a way that traditional narrative form cannot offer through its attachment to scientific objectivity and authority. Ethnographic poetry is rigorous, introspective, and humbling, laying bare experiences that ethnographic narrative can occlude with jargon. Ethnographic poetry is not simply eavesdropping on an open mic and ripping your interlocutors' experiences from them and into your published work. It is located within a larger practice of reciprocated communication.

Through writing poetry with and about my interlocutors, I examine the tensions within my own ethnographic practice. There are some experiences, some lines, some moments that I will never disclose out of respect for my interlocutors' agency and a rejection of anthropological conventions of what constitutes "sufficient" data (cf. Simpson 2007). I am a Black queer woman, and many of my interlocutors identify as Black queer women. Writing and telling our ordinary lived experiences through poetry allowed us to name that routine, often intergenerational, violence that influences the way we move through the world. Our pens and journals became the space where we could be vulnerable, where we did not have to press through or push on. In our poems, we did not deny ourselves the depth of our feeling. These poems also highlighted the places of difference and contradiction among us. My childhood as a sheltered, poor girl in South Carolina contrasted greatly with Harmony's and Mecca's lives in Baltimore. My current life as an anthropologist distanced me from the activism that characterized their daily lives. Though I view my own work as a political intervention in anthropological studies of Black women's and girls' lives, I would be naive to consider my own ethnographic monograph activism in and of itself. My Black feminist ethics of care compels me not only to create scholarship that brings analyzes my interlocutors' lives but also to couple my scholarship with a political practice that alters our lived conditions.

The only way to make my experiences intelligible to myself (and, to some extent, to others) was to write about them. I chose poetry as a method to help me heal from childhood abuse and intimate partner violence, as I no longer wanted to simply cope. Poetry, for me and my interlocutors, became the vehicle through which we processed our trauma and shared the ways we pressed forward. For us, poems articulated the event in a way that allowed us to feel control. We named the act of violence, maintaining the texture of life lived in the wake of rape and other forms of assault. Their poems shared that summer showcased the struggle and strength involved to build their own lives on their own terms, without turning to institutions to stitch them back together again. We know that traditional methods for justice always excluded us. In this way, our poetic practices fit into a long genealogy of Black women writers who wrote their violations out of obscurity to center their own healing, care, and liberation. Black enslaved women such as Harriet Jacobs (1861) and Mary Prince ([1831] 1997) wrote about the endemic sexual violence in slavery. Ida B. Wells, Rosa Parks, Fannie Lou Hamer, and others wrote about the erasure of sexual violence against Black women in activist movements during the twentieth century (Feimster 2009; McGuire 2011). Maya Angelou (1993) and June Jordan (2005) were Black women telling their own stories of violation through poetry and other literary works. We are among the latest generation of Black women writing ourselves from the margins to the center of our own lives and communities (where we have always been). Our work does not emerge from nothing like magic; instead, it stems from power.[4]

NOTES

1. All names have been changed to pseudonyms to protect my interlocutors' privacy.
2. Interpersonal violence advocates sometimes use "victim," "victim-survivor," and "survivor" interchangeably to describe those who are physically impacted by interpersonal violence. I use "victim" to describe a category of violated people, whose violations are upheld by state and legal definitions. "Victim-survivors," in my work, describes the ongoing condition and category of people living as survivors of sexual and/or gendered trauma while continuously experiencing violation.
3. I use quotation marks around "police brutality" here because I believe that all forms of policing are violent and brutal, so the term "police brutality" is redundant. For more, see Mariame Kaba's preface in *Invisible No More: Police Violence against Black Women and Women of Color* (2017).
4. Thank you to Destiny Hemphill, Brenda Onyango, and Lisa Del Sol for your insightful comments that brought this piece into being. I am indebted to your brilliance.

REFERENCES

Angelou, Maya. 1993. *I Know Why the Caged Bird Sings*. New York: Bantam Books.

Battle, Nishaun T. 2016. "From Slavery to Jane Crow to Say Her Name: An Intersectional Examination of Black Women and Punishment." *Meridians* 15 (1): 109–36.

Cole, Johnnetta B., and Beverly Guy-Sheftall. 2009. *Gender Talk: The Struggle for Women's Equality in African American Communities*. New York: One World/Ballantine.

Collins, Patricia Hill. 2000. *Black Feminist Thought: Knowledge, Consciousness, and the Politics of Empowerment*. New York: Routledge.

Crenshaw, Kimberlé W. 2012. "From Private Violence to Mass Incarceration: Thinking Intersectionally About Women, Race, and Social Control." *UCLA Law Review* 59 (6): 1418–72.

Crenshaw, Kimberlé W., Lori D. Patton, Chayla Haynes, and Terri N. Watson. 2016. "Why We Can't Wait: (Re)Examining the Opportunities and Challenges for Black

Women and Girls in Education (Guest Editorial)." *Journal of Negro Education* 85 (3): 194–98.

Davies, Carole Boyce. 1994. *Black Women, Writing, and Identity: Migrations of the Subject*. London: Routledge.

Davis, Dána-Ain, and Christa Craven. 2016. *Feminist Ethnography: Thinking through Methodologies, Challenges, and Possibilities*. Lanham, MD: Rowman and Littlefield.

Feimster, Crystal Nicole. 2009. *Southern Horrors: Women and the Politics of Rape and Lynching*. Cambridge, MA: Harvard University Press.

Freedman, Estelle B. 2013. *Redefining Rape: Sexual Violence in the Era of Suffrage and Segregation*. Cambridge, MA: Harvard University Press.

Garza, Alicia. 2014. "A Herstory of the #BlackLivesMatter Movement by Alicia Garza." *The Feminist Wire* (blog). October 7, 2014. www.thefeministwire.com.

Green, Erica L., Mark Walker, and Eliza Shapiro. 2020. "A Battle for the Souls of Black Girls." *New York Times*, October 1, 2020. www.nytimes.com.

Harris-Perry, Melissa V. 2011. *Sister Citizen: Shame, Stereotypes, and Black Women in America*. New Haven, CT: Yale University Press.

Hartman, Saidiya V. 1997. "Seduction and the Ruses of Power." In *Scenes of Subjection: Terror, Slavery, and Self-Making in Nineteenth-Century America*, 79–113. New York: Oxford University Press.

Jacobs, Harriet Ann. 1861. *Incidents in the Life of a Slave Girl*. Boston: Published for the Author.

James, Joy. 2013. "Afrarealism and the Black Matrix." *Black Scholar* 43 (4): 124–31.

Jordan, June. 2005. *Directed by Desire: The Collected Poems of June Jordan,* edited by Jan Heller Levi and Sara Miles. Port Townsend, WA: Copper Canyon.

Kaba, Mariame. 2017. Preface to *Invisible No More: Police Violence against Black Women and Women of Color*, edited by Andrea J. Ritchie, xi–xv. Boston: Beacon.

Lindsey, Treva B. 2015. "Post-Ferguson: A 'Herstorical' Approach to Black Violability." *Feminist Studies* 41 (1): 232–37.

Lorde, Audre. 1984. *Sister Outsider: Essays and Speeches*. Trumansburg, NY: Crossing.

McClaurin, Irma. 2001. Introduction to *Black Feminist Anthropology: Theory, Politics, Praxis, and Poetics*, edited by Irma McClaurin, 1–23. New Brunswick, NJ: Rutgers University Press.

McGuire, Danielle L. 2011. *At the Dark End of the Street: Black Women, Rape, and Resistance—A New History of the Civil Rights Movement from Rosa Parks to the Rise of Black Power*. New York: Vintage Books.

Mulla, Sameena. 2008. "There Is No Place like Home: The Body as the Scene of the Crime in Sexual Assault Intervention." *Home Cultures* 5 (3): 301–25.

———. 2014. *The Violence of Care: Rape Victims, Forensic Nurses, and Sexual Assault Intervention*. New York: New York University Press.

Mulla, Sameena, and Heather Hlavka. 2011. "Gendered Violence and the Ethics of Social Science Research." *Violence Against Women* 17 (12): 1509–20.

Prince, Mary. (1831) 1997. *The History of Mary Prince: A West Indian Slave*. Edited by Moira Ferguson. Rev ed. Ann Arbor: University of Michigan Press.

Richie, Beth. 2012. *Arrested Justice: Black Women, Violence, and America's Prison Nation*. New York: New York University Press.

Ritchie, Andrea J. 2017. *Invisible No More: Police Violence against Black Women and Women of Color*. Boston: Beacon.

Roberts, Dorothy E. 1999. *Killing the Black Body: Race, Reproduction, and the Meaning of Liberty*. New York: Vintage.

Romero, Regina. 2000. "The Icon of the Strong Black Woman: The Paradox of Strength." In *Psychotherapy with African American Women: Innovations in Psychodynamic Perspectives and Practice*, edited by Leslie C. Jackson and Beverly Greene, 225–38. New York: Guilford.

Sharpe, Christina Elizabeth. 2016. *In the Wake: On Blackness and Being*. Durham, NC: Duke University Press.

Simpson, Audra. 2007. "On Ethnographic Refusal: Indigeneity, 'Voice' and Colonial Citizenship." *Junctures: The Journal for Thematic Dialogue* (9): 67–80.

Spillers, Hortense J. 1987. "Mama's Baby, Papa's Maybe: An American Grammar Book." *Diacritics* 17 (2): 65–81.

Stallion, Megan Thee. 2020. "Why I Speak Up for Black Women." *New York Times*, October 13, 2020. www.nytimes.com.

Tynes, Brendane. 2020. "How Do We Listen to the Living?" *Anthropology News Website* (blog), August 31, 2020. www.anthropology-news.org.

Vargas, João Costa, and Joy A. James. 2013. "Refusing Blackness-as-Victimization: Trayvon Martin and the Black Cyborgs" In *Pursuing Trayvon Martin: Historical Contexts and Contemporary Manifestations of Racial Dynamics*, edited by George Yancy and Janine Jones, 193–203. Lanham, MD: Lexington Books.

Wallace, Michele. (1979) 2015. *Black Macho and the Myth of the Superwoman*. London: Verso.

3

Interwoven Violence

Gender-Based Violence, Haunting, and Violence Research in Milpa Alta, Mexico City

CATHERINE WHITTAKER

With a sigh, the elderly, unmarried Socorro showed me a photograph of her friend Teresa: a slender, rosy-cheeked seventeen-year-old of average height with sleek black hair and a feisty smile. Teresa had disappeared without a trace. Plagued with feelings of guilt, Socorro dreaded what might have happened. My ethnographic research on the southern border of Mexico City was haunted by this case. I needed to know what happened. For Socorro. For myself.

Interviewing people on their traumatic losses and experiences is ethically challenging, as it might trigger and even revictimize them. I could not simply interview Teresa's parents, given that they were not even opening up to their friends. More broadly, focusing on violence risks reducing people to their worst experiences. By starting this chapter with the example of Teresa, I may be contributing to a damaging, unidimensional perception that Indigenous women, and women from the Global South more broadly, are victims of gender violence. Yet, is it possible to study violence against women without already constructing women as victims in advance? This uncomfortable question cannot simply be avoided, as ignoring violence and the suffering caused by it would be unethical, too. I could not be indifferent to Socorro's torment.

Yet "anthropologizing" about Teresa's story, by trying to make sense of it in terms recognizable to the academy, is a way of distancing myself from the difficult emotions it conjured for Socorro and me. While many anthropologists have formed deep emotional bonds with their research subjects and collaborators, their writing too often seeks to *make sense*, rather than sense what was being made or undone in the moment of those encounters (cf. Stewart 2017). I suggest instead affectively as well as intellectually attending to what is being woven together or unraveled in research conversations and the intersubjective experiences that take place around these conversations. My research methodology grew from local knowledge priorities that foreground interweaving as a way of life. Here I provide some examples of interweaving and its ambivalences, from which I draw some general conclusions. Teresa's story will accompany us, as it did during my time living in Milpa Alta.

Living in Milpa Alta

For my doctoral research on local conceptualizations of violence against women, I spent fifteen months living in Santa Ana Tlacotenco, a small town in the macrocommunity of Milpa Alta (Nahuatl: Malacachtepetl Momozco or Momochco Malacatetipac; Farfán and Ángel 2008, 215). It consists of twelve pueblos and is the most rural of the sixteen boroughs of Mexico City, located to the south of its urban sprawl. I selected Milpa Alta as my field site because in 2015, at the time of my research, it reported the second-highest femicide rate among Mexico City's municipalities, and it shares a border with the State of Mexico, which reported the highest number of femicides in Mexico (OCNF 2015). In addition, this is where the most conservative variant of Nahuatl is spoken, the language of the Aztecs, which I had already begun to study and love in my undergraduate days.

I focused on cultural groups, which were predominantly composed of women past their reproductive age, and fully participated in their activities. This would normally seem like an unusual choice for a study on "violence against Indigenous women," but it had several methodological advantages. When I first arrived in Milpa Alta, as an unaccompanied, young, white foreign woman, it was easy to find male interview partners, who were accustomed to the role of the "stranger-handler." By contrast, many women initially treated me with suspicion because I was a stranger and because of my independence and my friendship with shaman's apprentices, which cast doubt on my moral qualities. This perception began to change when my interlocutors learned that I was an *europea*, not a *gringa*, and became involved in cultural revitalization groups. By participating in my friends' lives, marching along on Mexico's Independence Day and learning some Nahuatl, I slowly and somewhat clumsily wove myself into the social fabric. I also mobilized certain gendered scripts (Mazzei and O'Brien 2009). For example, after singing with a folkloric group at the Day of the Dead festivities of Santa Ana Tlacotenco, the town mayor thanked us and commented that I wore the traditional women's clothing "with dignity" and had even learned to weave. Therefore, joining cultural groups helped me to befriend potential interviewees and get to know well-loved traditions, as well as to earn and show respect. It was crucial to build relationships of trust before interviewing women on their experiences of violence or sharing my own.

By the time my friends began to joke that I had become a *santanera* (person from Tlacotenco), I realized that my perception had changed, too. I had changed. Having lost my faith after previous trauma, I nurtured a new sense of spirituality through my shared practice with local Catholics and the shaman's apprentices. For better and for worse, as it brought both joy and heartache, Tlacotenco had become a second home to me, and its people were no longer just (potential) research participants but my neighbors and, in some cases, loved ones—*seres queridos*. This affective entanglement was both unsettling and healing, as I address later.

The Problem of "Victimhood"

The women I met frequently discussed violence, femininity, and Indigeneity without being prompted, or feeling pressured to do so, and expressed a wide range of opinions. By not focusing my study on women's rights activists, health workers, social workers, or another group of people whose role is specifically defined in relation to violence against women, I was able to sidestep the pernicious ethnographic problem of inadvertently normalizing tropes that align specific, narrow roles of victim- and perpetratorhood in gender-based violence scenarios. In Milpa Alta and beyond, women rarely refer to themselves as "victims," in part, because they do not want their identity to be permanently defined by their negative experiences (Whittaker 2020). It is one thing to say that one has been victimized at specific points in one's life and quite another to be labeled a "victim." The problem arises not from the word "victim" itself but from the violence of categorization, which bestows the status of victimhood on some and refuses to recognize the victimhood of others, as Brendane Tynes points out (in chapter 2 of this volume).

My interlocutors consisted of both women who identified as having been "victims" in the past and those who never have, even if they did personally experience violence. For example, when discussing gender violence in general, Leona, a respected elder of the community, discussed the difficulties she had with her violent, hard-drinking husband but highlighted her active role in working through those problems and did not see herself as a victim. Magdalena, a young single mother, said that she finally decided never to return to her violent partner after attending a therapy group for women who had experienced intimate violence: "We shared many life stories, and I became aware of other women and said, 'Oh no!' I was one of the youngest women. I heard other women's life stories who had been with their husbands for fifteen, thirty years and who were vaguely thinking about leaving them. I said, 'No, I don't want that.'" Therefore, seeing that older women seemed unable to leave their husbands even after decades of abuse strengthened Magdalena's resolve not to be like them. When women did speak of victimhood, it was in the past tense, something they had overcome by directly fighting back or by finding the strength to verbally confront their abuser. Men were often more willing to accuse their wives of ongoing violence against them, perhaps because they were less afraid of the consequences of such disclosures. The medical doctor Adrián claimed that men are the victims of domestic violence just as often as women are. "It's 50 percent! Women, too, hit men, yell at them, and humiliate them." He claimed that machismo, rather than allowing men to dominate the relationship, only has the effect that men remain silent about the violence they suffer, and he added, "Women from these parts are very aggressive."

Yet, while several women advised me not to go out after 9 p.m., the town mayor and other men dismissed such claims, suggesting that I would be perfectly safe walking around even at 3 a.m. This difference in perceived vulnerability is a clear indicator that men in Tlacotenco are not actually exposed to the same levels of violence as women are. I took my female friends' advice seriously and accepted opportunities to walk together in the evening whenever possible. We were particularly careful not to walk alone in the period after an unknown person committed a femicide against a thirty-year-old woman in my neighborhood. Yet the only situations in which I felt directly threatened happened in the daylight. I was sexually harassed by one of my Nahuatl teachers when the two of us went walking in the forest once, and I experienced furtive groping on the overcrowded bus to Milpa Alta. Apart from those few occasions, the main threat in my Tlacontencan life were dogs, angrily defending the property of their owners, who often mistreated them. Some of my female friends carried sticks to fend them off.

Women and men who were still experiencing violence often could not speak about it but would communicate their experience in gestures and through their silence. Bety, a stout sexagenarian with whom I had spent many mirthful evenings singing and dancing, fell silent before our interview could even take off. Talking about her life was too difficult for her. From other women's and some of her own previous comments, I already knew she could not read, struggled economically, and had survived an abusive husband. Silence may be a sign of a woman's agentive hiding of pain. Not to recognize such embodied or verbal affirmations of pain is to become complicit in the violence that caused it (Das 2007, 55–57). Bety's silent story matters.

A more conventional approach to studying violence against women in Milpa Alta would have involved focusing on workers and service users at the local branch of a government agency dedicated to advancing women's rights and fighting violence against women. In that case, I would have worked with a sample of women who are much more willing to identify as "victims" than most. I instead organized my inquiry around local knowledge and experience priorities (TallBear 2014). This decision inevitably affected my loyalties and analysis, making me less critical of the cultural groups I was working with. While I was not blind to the ways in which such groups can contribute to sustaining gendered inequalities in Milpa Alta, I sought to give space to their often-misunderstood point of view and take it seriously. Thus, precisely because I took the intersecting structural vulnerabilities of Milpaltense women seriously, I sought to hold various perspectives in tension, speaking to and getting to know as many women, and also men, as possible.

Interweaving as Method

At the Milpaltense back-strap-loom weaving workshop I participated in, the mostly female apprentices described many motivations to me, including wanting to connect with their ancestral Nahua heritage and other women, as well as to experience the joy of learning a new skill, the challenge and privilege of mastering a highly respected and increasingly rare craft, and the tactile satisfaction of making garments of one's own design with one's own hands for oneself. Designs often featured Milpaltense flora and fauna and mythic motifs. Some of the women also highlighted that the repetitive motions of weaving were relaxing, providing an almost meditative escape from everyday stress. By meeting on a weekly basis and helping each other, the women soon became a tight-knit group. More than just a hobby or a line of work, weaving is a symbolic practice of great importance in Aztec philosophy (cf. Maffie 2014, 382–83) and in contemporary identity politics: its continued existence aids Milpaltenses in legitimizing Indigeneity-based rights claims.

Widening the application of weaving to social becoming and cultural production in general, I define "interweaving" as an ongoing, patterned practice of affectively harnessing relationships, material conditions, knowledge, and the imagination toward producing Milpaltense lifeworlds. It also involves integrating negative experiences and histories into people's lifeworlds. Yolotl, a forty-year-old artist whom I met at the class, said that weaving felt "Zen-like" and relaxing to her, though she also mentioned that this was not the case for her mother. She had been forced to weave by her grandfather as a child, so that she made her husband promise that she would never have to again. Weaving can feel wonderfully relaxing until it becomes painful for one's back and knees after several hours.

Literally and metaphorically, weaving describes a practice of skilled, rhythmic repetition that operates within a field of forces that cut across design, practitioner, and material (Ingold 2000, 342). Precisely because of its ambivalent nature, weaving is both an apt metaphor of and a vehicle for making social lifeworlds and feminine subjectivities. As an analytical concept, it works as an antidote to indiscriminate, existential "entanglement" or homogeneous visions of culture, which cannot account for the differences in the connections between humans and other beings and things—the differences in "what gets inside" and becomes part of the self (Roberts 2017). A person does not become the violence they have experienced, but they will often integrate those experiences into their fabric of self. Learning to weave is a profoundly social practice, as learners pay attention to both their own embodied actions and sensations and those of other learners and teachers around them (Csordas 1993, 139). In much the same way, through practices of narration and sharing, memories come to transcend the experience that they are based in and become social.

The Day Teresa Disappeared

Returning to Teresa, I finally wove her story together from several conversations with Socorro and filled in the gaps (cf. Jackson 2002, 57). At first, Teresa was the hope of her family. Her tough, hardworking mother, Rita, who had a strict upbringing, made sacrifices to put her daughters through school and expected them to perform well. Because Teresa had good grades, Rita would compare her older sister, Susana, to her disparagingly, which failed to motivate Susana to do better. Teresa's first romance was very innocent and sweet, with a younger boy who would wait for her by the church with a heart-shaped balloon.

However, things took a turn for the worse when Teresa started dating an older boy, who was not from their pueblo, a so-called *extracomunitario*— which for Tlacotencans is reason enough to question a person's values. He was also dealing drugs. Around that time, Teresa's grades were worsening. Socorro, whom Teresa affectionately called *mamá* because she acted as a mother-figure to her, told her to leave the guy, warning her that his actions could get her into jail, too. Teresa left him eventually. Then one night after dark, a group of six, consisting of four hooded men and two undisguised female *extracomunitarias*, dragged Teresa into a car by the main plaza and took her to the highway, where they beat her up. Her body was covered with bruises, and she could barely walk. Socorro suspected the ex-boyfriend of sending those thugs as an act of revenge. Teresa's parents appeared to know nothing of this event.

In February 2015, Teresa left her parents' home because her mother had told her that she had to either get good grades or get a job. So Teresa packed her things and brought them to Socorro's house on a Wednesday around noon, when both her parents were at work and would not notice. Socorro welcomed Teresa but informed her parents, so they would not worry. When Teresa saw her parents and her aunt Carmen approaching Socorro's house the next day, she ran away. This was the last they saw or heard of her.

Socorro feared that Teresa's parents' pride might have prevented them from declaring Teresa as missing. Her feelings of guilt over betraying Teresa's trust had already haunted her for seven months. Socorro anxiously awaited her return. After months without a word, this state of hypervigilance and pain weighed heavily on her. Teresa's parents also seemed to be privately suffering, as they withdrew from their social obligations and her father hit the bottle even harder than before. Yet they refused to even mention Teresa. This is why Socorro kept asking herself, Is Teresa dead or alive?

Haunting Uncertainty

Following Hélène Cixous, the blurring of life and death is precisely what makes haunting so "uncanny" and intolerable (1976, 543). Did Teresa run away, or was she forcibly "disappeared"? And what social context produces this kind of uncertainty? I was faced with the need to balance my desire to end Socorro's suffering and soothe my own anxiety in looking for an answer, while avoiding reopening Teresa's family's wounds.

An unspeakably terrible possibility haunting Socorro's, and subsequently my, imagination was that Teresa could have been trafficked, as she fit the profile of so many other disappeared women in Mexico. The International Organization for Migration estimates that each year twenty thousand people are trafficked in Mexico. Santa Ana Tlacotenco shares a border with the State of Mexico, where 1,238 women and girls were reported missing in 2011 and 2012 (Lakhani 2015). Of these, 53 percent were girls of Teresa's age or younger. Occasionally, missing girls are found alive or dead, but often, the cases remain unsolved. Moreover, although femicide is a legal category in Mexico, it is not often employed by the authorities. At the time of my research, the murder of a thirty-year-old Tlacotencan mother was not officially classified as a femicide, although it fulfilled the characteristics of sexual violence and humiliation. Even before this event, my older female friends avoided being outside at night. But the fear generated by living close to the scene of a femicide altered their general sense of safety even more. During the funeral mass, the priest warned that "big city" violence had finally arrived in rural Tlacotenco. In light of Tlacotenco's proximity to the perceived violent spaces of Mexico City proper and the State of Mexico and visible violence against women within Tlacotenco, it is understandable that Teresa's disappearance evoked a fear of nefarious possibilities in Socorro and me.

Seres queridos

While Socorro and I were both afraid, there were also differences, some of which were personal and others cultural. "For the secular humanist elites, ghosts can only be uncanny presences, returning to a space from which they had been banished by disbelief. For others, they are less uncanny than frightening, because real: expected, but only in their suddenness" (Morris 2008, 230). In my mind, Teresa existed in a space between life and death. Yet for Socorro, death was not the end of life but the beginning of a journey. No longer human, the *seres queridos*, the "beloved beings," as the dead are usually referred to, revisit the places they have been to in life, eventually traveling to the otherworld, a beautiful place of abundance. The otherworld is not entirely sealed from human perception and can be glimpsed through shamanic techniques. Every year, the dead return to the world of the living to visit their families on the Day of the Dead but may also make their presence felt on other occasions.

One time, Socorro saw a tall female figure standing behind me as I wrote notes in her house. She opined that it was a caring relative of mine checking up on me. In the light of day, this figure was invisible to me, but at night, "the possibility of spirits," as van de Port (2017) expresses it, bled into my ontological certainties, weaving itself into my consciousness. Local women often speak of dead beings in their midst in the same casual tone used when they gossip about the living. The perceivable presence of *seres queridos* from the otherworld was not disputed.

While the physically dead continue to be social actors, those who are physically alive can be socially "dead," in the sense of being shamed and rejected by their community to the extent that neither their physical nor metaphysical presence is tolerated (Mayblin 2011).[1] Such individuals are no longer subject to protection or punishment but are essentially left to live and die alone (Mayblin 2011). Because disappeared young women in Mexico are unlikely to be seen ever again, they are often assumed to be dead but cannot be mourned and celebrated on the Day of the Dead.

Hence, for Socorro and me, Teresa had an ambiguous status, somewhere between life and death, which made her a haunting preoccupation in a way that *seres queridos* and social rejects are not.

Accordingly, asking whether Teresa was dead or alive sets up a false opposition. She could have been clinically dead but socially alive.

From Haunting to Interweaving

Just as my haunting had begun with a photograph, it ended with another. While interviewing Carmen, Teresa's aunt and an assertive local politician, I looked at her family photos and noticed one with young girls. Carmen matter of factly explained that one was Teresa, who recently had a child and was living in a different pueblo. It turned out that Teresa was very much alive for Carmen but dead to her mother. I shared this with Socorro, who was relieved. Whether or not Teresa's parents know of my knowledge, and that I shared it with Socorro, is unknown to me, but thankfully we remain on good terms.

Being haunted by Teresa's story viscerally brought home to me that there is much at stake in declaring somebody's fate as "unknowable"—when someone disappears, almost always, somebody knows what happened. Therefore, the ongoing fascination with haunting in Latin American studies and anthropology bears certain risks. For example, Nils Bubandt recently described witchcraft in Buli, Indonesia, "as an experience that refuses to yield to language, understanding, or the senses" (2014, 54). Similarly, the Drug War and what is constructed as the violent, femicidal space of Mexico City in the imagination of many Tlacotencans constitute unspeakably frightening, alien realities. The logic of those spaces appears incomprehensible, as they are not governed by the same values as Milpa Alta. And yet, to claim that something is "unknowable" is to assume that certain realities are not only different from one's own but also a threat to it (cf. Ahmed 2000). Thus, the known is woven into the unknown, just as presence is in absence, and the real in the unreal. Crucially, to give up on searching for truth risks reifying the state of haunting and turning oneself into an instrument of the powers that produced this existential uncertainty—whether these powers are of the order of upset parents or of a femicidal state.

Instead of trying to make sense in a situation in which reason meets its limits, interweaving allowed me to foreground affective bonds. Socorro and I were led by affection in our search for the truth about Teresa, although we will never know the full story—nor is it our place to.

Unraveling

At my white, European, patriarchal university, I had been taught to think about "giving back" to my host community, as if we were going to have a contractual, clearly defined give-and-take relationship (see also Moore and Hofeller, chapter 4 in this volume). Yet when I asked Tlacotencans what they would like me to do in exchange for participating in my research, they merely expressed that I should *convivir*—live with them, as part of the community. So, I did. Having been emotionally enmeshed in Tlacotencan life made my departure difficult for my Tlacotencan friends and me. I was terrified of leaving, as it felt like cutting off part of myself. Back in Scotland, the severing continued, as I was instructed to purge from my ethnography any trace of the affective bonds that had produced it. Affect becomes affectation. Physical and affective alienation was followed by textual alienation. I began to unravel.

A few months after returning to the UK, I woke from a nightmare, feeling guilty. Then I remembered an anxious dream that Socorro had told me about, which expressed fear that other women might judge and reject her. As one dream spilled into another, I recognized my "survivor's guilt" over parachuting in to study violence against women in Mexico and then leaving to transform women's stories into data from the comfort of my office. What made me feel particularly guilty, however, was what we did share—the strong affective bonds we had formed—and my inability to honor these bonds properly. Inexcusably, various reasons (ranging from health and financial issues to work and family obligations) prevented me from returning to Mexico for three full years, though I did try to at least stay in touch with some people. When I finally did see my Tlacotencan friends again, I was apprehensive, preparing myself for their disappointment and rejection. Instead, I was overwhelmed to find that they celebrated my return. We ate mole, danced, sang, and took group photos together. Yet it was also clear that my absence had caused those who were closest to me pain. Socorro's sisters told me that she had been struggling with depression after my departure, having grown fond of our evening chats. When at last I called to say that I was coming to visit, Socorro said that she had been thinking of me that morning and joked about our closeness and "telepathic connection."

I felt utterly overwhelmed with happiness, gratitude, and regret, marveling at the perversity of practicing ethnography in the way I had been trained to, which seemed to involve systematic affective disengagement, for the sake of some colonialist fantasy of objectivity. For different reasons, I found myself unable to start a new life in Tlacotenco, but it has inextricably become a part of my being. Whenever I return to my loved ones there, it feels like weaving a part of myself together again.

Final Remarks

How can ethnographers avoid inadvertently normalizing tropes that align specific, narrow roles of victim- and perpetratorhood in gender-based violence scenarios? Instead of focusing on women's rights activists, or another group of people whose role is specifically defined in relation to violence against women, working with women-led cultural groups allowed me to center the local importance of weaving as a skill and a way of life. By adopting interweaving as an ethnographic method, I studied violence in the context of women's complex, often joyful, lives. I came to know women as skillful, active knowledge bearers, rather than as "living wounds" (Mookherjee 2015). However, the decisions I made in weaving together the haunting story of a young woman's disappearance show that this methodological approach is messy. To become a part of other people's lives, and for them to become a part of yours, means that shared feelings, loyalties, and obligations complicate the research process and may take it in unexpected directions. Rather than see this only as a problem, I would suggest that it offers an opportunity to rehumanize the dehumanizing tendencies of some ethnographic approaches that continue to be taught in certain parts of the anthropological world. Recognizing the importance of affect in violence research, drawing attention to the interrelatedness of uncertainties and facts, and tracing how "individual," "local" incidents of violence are connected to global intersecting structures of violence provide an entry point for understanding gender-based violence—an understanding that is necessarily incomplete, as women's experiences partially intersect, diverge, and shift, as we weave and unravel ourselves and each other.

NOTE

This research was generously funded by the University of Edinburgh, the Mexican Government (SRE), and the Royal Anthropological Institute.

1. Note that Mayblin's definition of social death differs from Patterson's (1982) original concept.

REFERENCES

Ahmed, Sara. 2000. *Strange Encounters: Embodied Others in Post-Coloniality*. London: Routledge.

Bubandt, Nils. 2014. *The Empty Seashell: Witchcraft and Doubt on an Indonesian Island*. Ithaca, NY: Cornell University Press.

Cixous, Hélène. 1976. "Fiction and Its Phantoms: A Reading of Freud's *Das Unheimliche* (The "Uncanny")." *New Literary History* 7 (3): 525–48, 619–45.

Csordas, Thomas J. 1993. "Somatic Modes of Attention." *Cultural Anthropology* 8 (2): 135–56.

Das, Veena. 2007. *Life and Words: Violence and the Descent into the Ordinary*. Berkeley: University of California Press.

Farfán Caudillo, and Miguel Ángel. 2008. "Milpa Alta: Aproximación bibliográfica." *Boletín del IIB* 8 (1–2): 213–319.

Ingold, Tim. 2000. *The Perception of the Environment: Essays on Livelihood, Dwelling and Skill*. London: Routledge.

Jackson, Michael. 2002. *The Politics of Storytelling: Violence, Transgression, and Intersubjectivity*. Copenhagen: Museum Tusculanum Press.

Lakhani, Nina. 2015. "The Women Vanishing without a Trace." *BBC News Online*, September 14, 2015. www.bbc.co.uk.

Maffie, James. 2014. *Aztec Philosophy: Understanding a World in Motion*. Boulder: University of Colorado Press.

Mayblin, Maya. 2011. "Death by Marriage: Power, Pride, and Morality in Northeast Brazil." *Journal of the Royal Anthropological Institute* 17 (1): 135–53.

Mazzei, Julie, and Erin E. O'Brien. 2009. "You Got It, So When Do You Flaunt It? Building Rapport, Intersectionality, and the Strategic Deployment of Gender in the Field." *Journal of Contemporary Ethnography* 38:358–83.

Mookherjee, Nayanika. 2015. *The Spectral Wound: Sexual Violence, Public Memories, and the Bangladesh War of 1971*. Durham, NC: Duke University Press.

Morris, Rosalind. 2008. "Giving Up Ghosts: Notes on Trauma and the Possibility of the Political from Southeast Asia." *Positions* 16 (1): 229–58.

OCNF (Observatorio Ciudadano Nacional del Feminicidio). 2015. "La situación del feminicidio en México." Presentation slides on the OCNF website. http://observatoriofeminicidio.blogspot.co.uk.

Roberts, Elizabeth S. 2017. "What Gets Inside: Violent Entanglements and Toxic Boundaries in Mexico City." *Cultural Anthropology* 32 (4): 592–619.

Patterson, Orlando. 1982. *Slavery and Social Death: A Comparative Study*. Cambridge, MA: Harvard University Press.

Stewart, Kathleen. 2017. "In the World That Affect Proposed." *Cultural Anthropology* 32 (2): 192–98.

TallBear, Kim. 2014. "Standing with and Speaking as Faith: A Feminist-Indigenous Approach to Inquiry [Research Note]." *Journal of Research Practice* 10 (2): article N17. http://jrp.icaap.org.

van de Port, Mattjis. 2017. "The Possibility of Spirits." *Journal of Anthropological Films* 1 (1): e1316.

Whittaker, Catherine. 2020. "Felt Power: Can Indigenous Mexican Women Finally Be Powerful." *Feminist Anthropology* 1 (2): 288–303.

4

The Language of Dissent

A Conversation between a Researcher and Participant-Turned-Collaborator on Studying Domestic Violence

DAWN MOORE AND STEPHANIE HOFELLER

DAWN:

This Is for You.

For all who research gender-based violence (GBV) and are committed to do so without enacting research violence. I want us to have this conversation publicly because, if we are to truly explore the embodiments and entanglements of researching GBV, we need to hear from and give voice to the people who are the subjects of our research. Before I met Stephanie, I only paid lip service to these convictions (cf. Mulla 2014; Petillo 2015). Now they embody me, and I am entangled in them.

I invite you to "listen in" as two willful women (Ahmed 2014), who are in many ways privileged but not always lucky, explore who we are to each other and what our work, intended or unintended, does to and for each of us as it challenges the scripted paths of research.

STEPHANIE:

This Isn't for You.

This is for my children. Everything I do is for them. I am their mother.

Don't worry, it is not for their eyes only. So, if you happen to be reading this and you are not my children, you aren't invading our privacy. But since, as of today, they're not allowed to even know that I am their mother, their once and future questions remain my priority. If I end up answering yours, too, all the better. Knowledge is power . . . knowledge of the truth, that is. Truth is what I swore to tell as part of the little quid pro quo with "fate" that brings me, alive and well, if not whole, to here and now and to this opportunity to "speak," more literally, to write.

But what is this I'm writing? Although the title is "A Conversation," it's actually an academic paper, specifically about our collaborative relationship, including my feelings about it, and feelings are complicated, feelings aren't objective.

DAWN:
Funnily I also don't know what I am writing because all my training, all of my methodological rigor, never prepared me for a relationship like ours. Even wandering into the more personalized methodologies of anthropology (where I am only a tourist and don't speak the language), I struggle to define who we are or what we do. I know we see the same deep injustices when the state enters into a woman's life with the master key of "helping" only to wreak havoc, take control, and overthrow any sense of agency she might have. I know that we both read what happened to you and what happened to me in the same way, as grave and relentless acts of state violence, but I don't know what this is called when researcher and subject become collaborators (or conspirators). So let's focus on the actions, not the definitions. Let's meander and discover, knowing we can't bookend this because the story is constantly unfolding. To do anything else would suggest that we can define what we are only coming to know. Maybe when we are finished, I will know what to call us, but I don't see anything that looks like "finished" happening anytime soon. I have given up on trying to finish and instead bought a one-way ticket on your wild ride.

STEPHANIE:
Excellent. Because innovation and creativity don't only make moving works of art . . . they also yield paradigm-shifting scientific discoveries. Innovation is, by definition, unconventional.

And yet few but The Academy would call forefronting your subject's point of view an unconventional method. In fact, it is the opinion of The Academy (being by and for the elite) that is unconventional, not the other way around.

Furthermore, by employing this "unconventional" approach (more accurately defined as "conventional"), you and I have found new answers to many important questions asked about the violence in our society.

From a point of view that is perhaps on the edge of convention, perhaps in the eye of the storm, we see the problems that are, at the behest of The State or The Crown, analyzed by the academy and, time and time again, find ourselves indicting as cause, not the victim, not even the perpetrator, but instead hierarchy itself.

Dawn, since you literally started the conversation that isn't a conversation but is, let's begin again as you began, with an introduction to the story of how we "accidentally" entered into our, as yet to be defined, collaboration.

DAWN:

In 2015, reacting to widespread concern over "no drop" policies and vigorous, "evidence-based" or "victimless" prosecution of domestic violence, Rashmee Singh and I began a study to explore the collection and use of evidence, particularly visual evidence, by the criminal justice system in order to examine the government's response to domestic violence and its effect, positive or negative, on its victims.

As substantiated in the literature (Bumiller 2008; Lemieux 2017; Thuma 2019; hooks 1995), our research revealed a considerable dissonance between the experiences and needs of victimized people and police responses. Police were trained to engage in a process of rapid evidence collection including pressuring victims into making sworn vide statements that could, in criminal proceedings, be used against or in place of an actual victim on the stand.

Taking inspiration from Richard Ericson and Kevin Haggerty's (1997) work on surveillance, Singh and I thought this through as creating a data double, a victim of pure virtuality, more compliant than the actual victim and more predictable in their affect.

Singh and I published preliminary findings. One article, "Seeing Crime, Feeling Crime: Visual Evidence, Emotions, and the Prosecution of Domestic Violence" (2017), included review of a case from the United States, *State of West Virginia v. Peter Lizon* (2012). The case pivoted not on the noncompliant victim's testimony but on photographs taken of the victim's body. The scant portion of the record available, not including the actual photographs, was enough to reveal that the "victim" had been further victimized by unwanted state intervention.

Shortly after that first article was published, I received an email, the kind that makes a researcher's heart stop.

> Dr. Moore,
> My name is Stephanie Hofeller (formerly Stephanie Lizon). . . .
> I am very curious to read your paper and also, if you're interested, discuss the case.

The worries that, as a GBV researcher, are always in the back of my mind rushed forward. Perhaps you felt exploited or misrepresented. With a rush of fear, I called; you picked up.

Stephanie, you, as always, had done your homework. You knew that I was a survivor of sexual assault and, more acutely, a survivor of the press and the police work and all the empty promises of help and justice that came quickly on the heels of my assault. I remember your words exactly: "I know that you've had your own experiences with this shit too."

We had Tarana Burke's moment of "seeing" each other on common ground of shared experiences of violence (Burke 2018). But still I was waiting for the judgment. Did you agree or disagree with what I had written about your case? Knowing I could never see through your eyes, did I at least fairly represent "your truth" (Mohanty 1988)?

STEPHANIE:

My life was profoundly and positively changed by the single, defining moment that I discovered, online, the abstract of "Seeing Crime."

A search on "Lizon" had returned your resource list, which included "State of WV v Peter Lizon." Because of the ridiculous amount of press on my "captivity" and "forced childbirth in chains" (A.P. Morgantown, WV, 2012, etc., etc., etc.), that is, the fabricated fiction of my "life," I was used to reading about "me"—more animal than human, not even capable of opinion, a creature who had only the machinery of reflex and reaction, panic, fear . . . submission. But your abstract, alone, implied a different point of view. The theory of "data double" as antagonistic to victim was the first sentence I had ever read that even suggested the possibility that anyone in the world might understand, much less share, my opinion.

In retrospect, that moment feels to me more like our first meeting than anything else because it was, in fact *my* moment of "seeing" common ground.

I knew enough about academic research to know that hearing from me might make you uncomfortable. How appropriate that it was the issue of ownership (I could only access the abstract online) that goaded me to reach out. Your name was first (hierarchy, again), so I knew that it was "your" paper. . . .

I sent that first email on the morning of October 9, 2017. Less than an hour later, I got a call from "Ottawa." Thrilled, I picked up.

Your prompt reply by phone rather than automated email was already a demonstration of respect on a level to which I was not accustomed. It kinda got us off on the right foot.

You emailed me the entire article as well as notes on a paper in progress, "How She Appears." By the end of the week, we had established a solid line of communication.

But phone and email were still terrifying weaknesses in my lines of defense. You offered to fly to the US, but I rejected that offer, explaining how political motives had driven my persecution and how my father's powerful position had influenced it.

Although that assertion confounded you (not Rashmee, who was raised in the States), in late November, you brought me to Canada so I could speak freely.

It had been less than a year since I ran from my, then, only recently divorced ex-husband with literally nothing. Surviving meant hiding, not only from him but also from my influential and abusive father and, with him, my entire family, so I had very few resources. Adhering to my strict safety plan, you fought valiantly so that I could be compensated without records of my identity. Perhaps this was the first phase of the pushback that you experienced, stubbornly refusing to let this opportunity pass us by.

While attempting to answer your question about wrong-gotten story parts, I caught myself in the first, major, compulsive loop of redefining what, exactly, I wanted to say about our collaboration.

We eventually agreed that, from my lived experience and a four-thousand-page-plus record, no summary briefer than the modest sixteen pages of "Forty-Five Colour Photographs . . ." (Moore and Hofeller 2019) could possibly be worth writing, much less including in this piece. With that cut went the corrections, some of which, I'll admit, I was surprised I had to make.

What remained was my question to you: "Dawn, I have yet to have a lawyer or friend or colleague or therapist that hasn't at some point revealed that broad and/or critical elements of my story were missing or wrong in their recollection. What is it about my story that makes everyone get it not quite right? Is it empathy?"

You were quick to answer that. Early on, you were encumbered by disbelief, but still you (and I) wondered what had fueled it. Was it your Canadian legal lexicon, white privilege, class privilege, a position of authority?

DAWN:
All of the above and maybe also the simple fact that your story is among the worst I have ever heard. And I don't mean the violence in and of your marriage; I mean the violence done to you by all the helpers and advocates, all the ones who promise justice and safety and another chance (Bumiller 2008; Mulla 2014). But as you told them, I checked and rechecked every detail of each larger-than-life chapter in your narrative. Not once did your telling fail to match the evidence. And everything I found out left me with more questions.

All justice systems are rigged, but the matrix of law that descended on you struck me as almost deliberately impenetrable; and there were so many moving parts that I still struggle to keep them all in view, regularly categorizing details as "not relevant," only to have you correct me later.

STEPHANIE:
Whether or not you are aware, I assure you that the officers of the court are aware of how unimportant those small details seem. That is precisely why they labor them in secret (family) court. A victim of the court will spend some time, babbling about these details, telling a bizarre story about a finding based on them . . . until shame shuts them up.

But given what you've not only studied and witnessed but literally suffered, it seems odd that my story would surprise you. Are you sure you were that cynical?

DAWN:
Maybe not cynical but certainly skeptical—occupational hazard. That instinct to doubt is part of how the academy institutionalized me. Sure, I believe survivors; but belief is not rigor, and so I have to double check and

check again. Disregarding the academy's standards is less available the less privilege you have, especially when your research is on/with women who have been victimized—considered an inherently untrustworthy bunch in so many circles (Epstein and Goldman 2019). In my world, even with the privilege of being white, born middle class, and having success-fully navigated the academy's markers of progress, there always has to be proof. Researchers can never just believe, even when we say we do.

Thinking on it now, that skepticism lessened as I got to know you, not only because you established yourself as reliable but because you became more "real" to me.

So there is something about objectification here.

I spent weeks puzzling over your case with you positioned as an ab-straction. Then you emailed, and I began to find you behind the infa-mous victim. The flesh made real—like an inversion of the data double. It was unexpected and staggering.

STEPHANIE:

Yes, I am not only living rather than dead but also stubborn in my re-fusal to be objectified. And this conversation is convincing me that my refusal to be objectified is the root cause of the aphasia-like phenom-enon I've widely observed. I suspect that some of your "skepticism" was actually a subconscious effort to compartmentalize and quiet the disso-nance of your accidental empathy. Knowing that I'm not an object, you can no longer objectify me. But, you see, none of us are objects, actually. And upon reflection, I am finally able to articulate why your telling of my story, details included, was so important, not just to my feelings, not just to the accuracy of your study, but to my literal fate:

Your authority lends you default credibility. Each time your telling of the narrative diverges from mine, it is my credibility that erodes in the eyes of the world, especially in the eyes of the court, with all of its awe-some, destructive power (Brodsky and Pivovarova 2016).

My lack of credibility was the sum total of the "merits" of the case against my parental rights and was proven, to "reasonable belief," one small detail at a time as a host of authorities recalled and contradicted me, even contradicted each other.

But you knew that this had happened to me, even before I was "real." What's different now? How did your understanding develop?

DAWN:

When you came into the work, I had no model to follow for how to ethically develop a relationship like ours. I found myself maintaining the sort of distance that my training deemed imperative to guard ethics (and ultimately guard against liability). But this did not sit right with me in the long term. Anthropologists immerse themselves in studied communities (cf. Mulla 2014; Petillo 2015). Surely a researcher and participant can become collaborators.

I wrote to the president of my university explaining that I had to break all the rules of my granting council because I needed to send you money with no paper trail. My ethics office was helpful. My president was not entirely happy, and the administrators decidedly had their noses out of joint. I did not apologize for not following the rules. I insisted that the rules were the problem; and eventually, by the power of academic freedom or simply tenacious women wearing them down, they caved, and you were "hired" on as a collaborator. But always, we kept you on the down-low.

STEPHANIE:

I was and still am acutely aware of Carleton University's ambivalence. Even as the revelations that followed my father's death grew my fame and with it my credibility, it seemed to gain me nothing with your Academy . . . any Academy.

But "wearing them down" is how I, and in fact women in general, have accomplished anything in this interminable, intolerable patriarchy.

We are so often underestimated that we turned it to our advantage. We retreated into the mother mind that exists outside of chronological time, and we studied patience. Rather than exasperate and pace, we continue our efforts, long after a powerful man would have resigned or declared war.

DAWN:

Well, you are my model of tenacity—in every way and especially in sticking with this work. You started doing so much more than simply working on your own case. How would you define what you and I are doing now? And no, you can't just say "revolution"!

STEPHANIE:

Oh, but I *can* just say, "revolution," and I do.

I say "revolution" because it is our very survival. It is the only thing we can in good conscience say if we want the children to live, rather than die. The unsustainable hierarchy sustained itself for millennia by stealing from the future . . . but they are out of future. All along, the future they stole from was We, Here, Now.

I say "revolution" because it is already under way. If you look up and listen, remember . . . you can hear it now. It is a revolution for the truth of our existence, as only with truth can there be justice. That truth is equality.

What you and I are doing is pulling off a coup.

DAWN:

Okay, I am with you in the revolution. But I still get anxious when I wage my minirevolts, even with my golden handcuffs of full professorship. And that anxiety is important. I don't want to lose it. It keeps me vigilant, and because of the power dynamic, I need to be vigilant.

STEPHANIE:

Your anxious vigilance won't be necessary if you see that power dynamic for the illusion that it is. Faith in the power of their imposed hierarchy is what causes the empathy-dissonance tune-out. If you regard me as the equal you know I am, your conscience will quiet down, and you can just listen to me. That empowers me to defend myself.

And despite your anxiety, you did, from the beginning, want to do something revolutionary . . . I remember, you told me.

DAWN:

But the revolution I imagined here was more modest. Traditionally we academics are trained to extract information and claim ownership of it regardless of how "connected" we claim to be to our research participants.

What I most wanted to do was upend the proprietorial terms, to give you ownership.

Do you own this work? Does it feel like it is yours?

STEPHANIE:

It does feel like mine, yes, regardless of how the academy marginalizes me and prevents my ownership in more literal ways. But even more than mine, this work feels like ours. In truth, we share ownership. We "saw" each other, not only as survivors but as willful women, coconspirators against inequality.

The academy demands hierarchy; but instead, we give it anarchofeminism (Kowal 2019), or more to the point, we give it Anarchy.

Objectivity, we see, will never find the truth about anything that isn't an object. Anarchy, being equality, resonates as truth. And this work now belongs to everybody.

The Academy, the better to lay claim even to my condemnation of its existence, demands I summarize, knowing that with its blunt language in its narrow time, I cannot.

Instead, I summarize in the language of dissent: it is metaphor; it is myth, poetry, and song.

It is a poem we can memorize, a song we can sing.

It is a secret song like the ones that I sang to my children, while we played in front of the one-way mirror as they watched, assessing my capacity to be what I already was—their mother.

They were prayers so beautiful that the younglings knew that we did not sing to El, even though we called his name, Yahweh, Jehovah, Muhammad, the Christ. The oppressors recorded, hoping I would fear. They noted every word I spoke to my children and called all of it heresy. But the songs I sang . . . I sang of love and revolution, so they wouldn't bother to listen, or if they listened, they would not understand.

Mojko, moj, they chastised me for saying it with words, but in song, they did not hear me telling you, my boy, that, someday, you would come home.

The system can't be fixed, and everyone knows it.

"How can I exit the script of the oppressed, within a structure whose foundation is built on my submission?" (Moore and Hofeller 2018, 87).

They forced our mother to her knees and, then, found her back so strong that they could build a tower upon it, up to the sun. Legend has it that their vanity cursed us to melodrama and babble. But the mother mind remembered, and so we all remembered, as there was never yet a living "man" who did not dwell within a mother, not even the "first" one (what a desperate lie).

I remembered, and then I remembered again. I remembered their deception, age upon age. And the vision of their blasphemous betrayal was everywhere, and I was enraged.

They dragged me to their court, to answer for my knowledge, like Eve . . . with that tree.

My rage was visible from quite a distance, it seems . . .

Because when you and Rashmee theorized that my attitude in *West Virginia v. Peter Lizon* was due not to "Stockholm," "Battered Wife," or any other syndrome but rather to my very own intelligent and willful plan for my own and my own children's life, you were correct.

Those in the academy wondering about how we subjects feel about being observed but not listened to, I'll speak for myself and every one of those subjects I ever met:

We see you, and we loathe you, and we find your amateur-night-at-the-strip-club fascination with our sex lives disgusting (Doe 2004). We wonder how you can claim to be feminists, while encouraging victim blame in your thorough examination of victims and your shoulder-shrugging dismissal of the rehabilitation of abusers? Is it not "boys will be boys," implying some lack of consent?! Objectifying and fetishizing the abuser does the same to the abused . . . and worse.

How can you wonder if our attitudes are relevant but neglect to ever ask us what our attitudes are? How can you wonder about the ethics of involving us, when the very question itself is a demonstration of how the sexist oligarchs stratify us, exaggerating the difference between women of privilege and the rest? Speaking from a position of "privilege" regained after decades of "real life," I can tell you that advocating for all women involves exactly that, and advocating for all women means advocating for men as well.

It means advocating for equality, not "special" crimes for "special" people. How can anyone tell me that violence against my daughter is a greater crime than violence against my son?!

If you can't study the men who lay hands on me, then why are you studying me? Perhaps you don't really want to help, just add to the expensive literature on a topic that, in truth, has a one-sentence answer: the problems you examine are your own creation.

But isn't it cute that y'all mistook me for a lab rat, just because I turned my back on abusive men, leaving my share of our wealth behind . . . temporarily . . . ?

Wealthy women do *not* have to stay at a DV shelter or find themselves at the mercy of angry social workers. They can set themselves up in a condo, hire a lawyer, and see a therapist of their choice. Confidentiality is something you have to buy.

Just as the kind of drug addict who can maintain the appearance of a normal life, the unseen victim is almost always, simply, a wealthy one. These are the victims who purposefully stay under your radar, so they don't appear in your research.

If y'all are truthfully worried about "taking advantage" of your position as professionals, then don't do studies in DV shelters that have control groups that work for free. Don't collude with the criminal state, with "funding" as a justification. Don't thrive in a society that favors greed and obedience and tolerance for the suffering of others, then adopt our children who live because nature favors traits that hierarchy distorts to preserve itself: courage into arrogance, stamina into cruelty, strength into violence, memory into hatred.

Halt your specious search for commonality among victims. How about looking for the commonality in abusers, instead?

Don't speak for me without my permission, please, especially if forced silence is the only reason I do not speak for myself. And please, don't pretend that you are unaware that criminalizing behavior only glamorizes it and that women have to be brainwashed before they become defenseless.

DAWN:

I want to take these paragraphs and make them mandatory reading for all social science methods courses. What you are saying about the assumptions made and violence carried out by researchers needs saying. Like racism, we see it, although we often don't realize what we are seeing, unless of course we are the ones experiencing the racism (or sexism or homophobia or transphobia or any other systemic or personalized target of hate in this world); then everything is crystal clear but unspeakable. Researchers like me who fashion themselves as anti-gender-based-violence advocates are capable of incredible violence and exploitation. We are directed to it. I pay you $50, and you tell me about your suffering for a few hours, and then I walk away with weak offers that you can "give feedback" or read over your interview transcript or whatever, knowing that I will never see you again, probably never be able to find you again. That was my experience until I met you. It will probably be my pattern again; but you created a rupture, and now that I know it is possible, I will continue to seek out the weaknesses in prescribed "best practices" of research.

STEPHANIE:

Yes, research! The question is not, "In which conditions will a human thrive?" but, rather, "How much failure to thrive can a human withstand?"

The Academy teaches that "clients" are not entirely human. No matter who you are, no matter who I am, your title guarantees you the power . . . oh, I'm sorry, burdens you with the power that overwhelms my faculties, robbing me of the ability to consent.

But if I cannot give consent, I can't revoke it, either. Now that is terrifying.

But I mentioned that being underestimated can become an advantage. Well, it has worked out rather well for me. They underestimate my children, too. It will only make it easier for them to find me . . . no bullshit court order necessary. Nature herself will compel them to find me. I sing to them in their dreams.

With me, alive or dead, they will find evidence of their stolen legacy and take it back.

Academy, tell the ethics board not to worry about taking advantage of me. It is I who took advantage of you. I can still count on the narcissism of the oligarchy to preserve its own product. What better record than "The Record"?

So, let The Record show I am mother to all the world's children . . . I cry for all of them. I could not be left unsupervised to raise my own, two, living children?

So be it. So, instead, I will "corrupt" generations against your tyranny. Instead, I will lead a revolution.

DAWN:

You have injected me with the spirit of revolution, and in that vein, I don't want to repackage you. What happens if you generate the words and I curate quietly in the background? We originally agreed that I was your witness, but I am not sitting by idly watching and taking notes. I'm in this with you—not just for research, though the research continues, but also for the humanity of using my power and privilege to try to help. We are rebuilding your case file, we are finding advocates, we are talking through problems and concerns. I worry with you about your abuser's new charges. I worry about you when I don't hear from you for a while, and none of that is rigorous research. It is friendship. And in declaring us friends, do I risk my own credibility? I guess the cat is already out of the bag, so here I am witnessing and listening and still on occasion disbelieving but also ready to be your credibility as long as our friendship/collaboration has not stripped me of mine.

STEPHANIE:

The quieter you are, the more likely that my name, sans initials, will again be misspelled (Moore and Hoffeler [sic]). Aphasia again.

But, if readers want to cross-reference my stories with my late father's exploits, they'll have to spell it H-O-F-E-L-L-E-R.

I'll endorse the New Yorker's piece (Bethea 2019) and leave the rest (including citations of another Dr. Hofeller, my mother, Kathleen) to the curious and save my stories for another day . . . or another paper.

Peace, y'all.

REFERENCES

Ahmed, Sara. 2014. Willful Subjects. Durham, NC: Duke University Press.

Bethea, Charles. 2019. "A Father, a Daughter, and the Attempt to Change the Census." New Yorker, July 12, 2019. www.newyorker.com.

Brodsky, Stanley, and Ekaterina Pivovarova. 2016. "The Credibility of Witnesses." In The Witness Stand and Lawrence S. Wrightsman, Jr., edited by Cynthia Willis-Esqueda and Brian H. Bornstein, 41–52. New York: Springer.

Bumiller, Kristin. 2008. In an Abusive State: How Neoliberalism Appropriated the Feminist Movement against Sexual Violence. Durham, NC: Duke University Press.

Burke, Tarana. 2018. "Me Too Is a Movement, Not a Moment." TED Talks, November 30, 2018. www.ted.com.

Doe, Jane. 2004. The Story of Jane Doe. Toronto: Vintage Canada.

Epstein, Deborah, and Lisa A. Goodman. 2019. "Discounting Women: Doubting Domestic Violence Survivors' Credibility and Dismissing Their Experiences." University of Pennsylvania Law Review 167 (2): 399–461.

Ericson, Richard, and Kevin Haggerty. 1997. Policing the Risk Society. Toronto: University of Toronto Press.

hooks, bell. 1995. Killing Rage: Ending Racism. New York: Henry Holt.

Kowal, Donna M. 2019. "Anarcha-Feminism." In The Palgrave Handbook of Anarchism, 265–79. Cham, Switzerland: Palgrave Macmillan.

Lemieux, Jamilah. 2017. "Weinstein, White Tears and the Boundaries of Black Women's Empathy." Cassius, November 2, 2017. https://cassiuslife.com.

Mohanty, Chandra. 1988. "Under Western Eyes: Feminist Scholarship and Colonial Discourses." *Feminist Review* 30 (1): 61–88.

Moore, Dawn, and Stephanie Hofeller. 2019. "'Forty-Five Colour Photographs': Images, Emotions and the Victim of Domestic Violence." In *Emotions and Crime: Towards a Criminology of Emotions*, edited by Michael Hviid Jacobsen and Sandra Walklate, 79–95. London: Routledge.

Moore, Dawn, and Rashmee Singh. 2017. "Seeing Crime, Feeling Crime: Visual Evidence, Emotions, and the Prosecution of Domestic Violence." *Theoretical Criminology* 22 (1): 116–32.

Mulla, Sameena. 2014. *The Violence of Care: Rape Victims, Forensic Nurses and Sexual Assault Intervention*. New York: New York University Press.

Petillo, April D. J. 2015. "Sex Trafficking of Native Peoples: History, Race, and Law." In *Applying Anthropology to Gender-Based Violence: Global Responses, Local Practices*, edited by Jennifer Wies and Hillary Haldane, 93–106. Lanham, MD: Lexington Books.

Thuma, Emily L. 2019. *All Our Trials: Prisons, Policing, and the Feminist Fight to End Violence*. Urbana: University of Illinois Press.

PART II

Being

Reflective Entanglements and (Academic) Violence by Another Name

In part 1 of this volume, contributors wrote about the processes of naming the impacts of doing their work while intimately aware of the challenges of their interlocutors' lives. Naming involves the shifting ability to identify emotions and sensations across social identities/bodies to understand how we intersect to cocreate different vulnerabilities, demands, or complicities. Researcher and participant lives intersect in numerous ways, and the contributors in part 1 made note of how those intersections gave them an enhanced perspective from which to witness gender-based violence *differently*. The authors highlighted where embodied methodological approaches, as an adaptive form of feminist methodological praxis, positively impacted their ability to get into or conceptualize their research projects. They also pinpointed where an embodied methodology allowed them to remain expansive in the work by giving them access to new perspectives that were unavailable to them previously or through other methodology.

The experiences shared and reflected in these chapters mirror a conversation that occurred years ago between two gender violence researchers. These two women of color brought years of experience working in Black, Indigenous, and/or people of color (BIPoC) communities, maneuvering responses to gender and sexual violence to their scholarship. As academics, they now worked within and for communities that institutions and agencies had labeled "hard to reach" just ten years prior. Their conversations, one of which is excerpted here, intimately informed the present collection.

"I mean, I've survived some difficult moments, . . . both in the academy and in my [personal] life. I know how dark and difficult and inspiring and uplifting it can be. You've had those moments, in your own way, too. So, why should we trust anyone to represent that who hasn't recognized that on some personal level as well?"

"Yeah. While it is important to understand multiple angles, why should we uphold one—objectivity—above awareness of what it means to live, physically, with any of this reality?"

"Exactly. As a subject who, say, finally has a chance to have my story told with at least some of my meaning given to it, why would I just give that to anyone, . . . even if they have a degree, . . . even if they have connections?"

"I don't know. Knowing what my experiences have been like, I don't know that I would share the 'true-true' with anyone who didn't have some kind of 'skin in the game,' as they say."

In many ways, these two scholars were discussing the reasons why methods such as feminist ethnography, a method that lends itself well to embodied methodology, are appealing. The commitment to documenting the intersectional, lived experiences of participants, attention to power differentials, and a commitment to social justice is at the heart of Christa Craven and Dána-Ain Davis's (2013) work described in *Feminist Activist Ethnography: Counterpoints to Neoliberalism in North America*. The excerpted conversation reveals the tension between researcher expectations around revelation and speech and about what is shared (or can be shared) in our public work (Stacey 1988), and our interlocutors' expectations for advocacy (Davis 2013) or a different kind of present, nonhierarchical listening (Tynes, chapter 2 in this volume; Moore and Hofeller, chapter 4 this volume).

But the tensions stem from more than method as technique; they illustrate Sandra Harding's (1987) point about the entanglement of epistemology and methodology, discussed in chapter 1. Why might someone even use feminist activist ethnography? The subtle ideas in this short exchange above illustrate the contextual drivers central to embodied methodology and entanglement. Those drivers pivot at the spaces where, as researchers, they have learned the vocabulary of their actions that operate beyond and above language. Embodied methodology requires a recognition of the multiple contexts in which knowledge is produced, shared, gained, wielded, and understood. It requires reflection and recognition of being witness to others and its impact, just as it requires recognition of how external concepts are projected onto that witnessing. Framing one's work through embodied methodology essentially requires dislocation and discomfort.

April Petillo (2020) has elaborated elsewhere about the politics of listening through the discomfort of encountering others' lived realities. This works to unsettle oneself out of the safe, pseudoimpartial role of observer and into a self-awareness that often pushes against the academic institutional norm. Heather R. Hlavka (2019) has similarly argued that the inability or unwillingness of researchers and others to listen to young people's experiences of harm amounts to epistemic violence (Dotson 2011) in its objectifying, essentializing, and silencing effects. The push to disrupt and transform categorization of our interlocutors provides opportunity to engage in reflective embodied listening. In its most basic form, to listen reflectively is to focus on understanding another's point or perspective so deeply that you can offer that idea back and confirm that you have correctly received it. Reflective embodied listening takes things a step further to require researchers to also listen intently to their own knowledge and understanding of what has been conveyed to them through their personal reactions, feelings, and thoughts. Such intentional, multilayered listening is sometimes uncomfortable, but it is a necessary reality in gender violence research—where issues such as shame, ostracization, blame, shock, and fear easily determine what an interlocutor chooses to share, whether they identify as a victim/survivor or not.

On the one hand, there is the opportunity to open additional conversational spaces between researchers and interlocutors/participants. This can lead researchers to a better understanding of the nuances of violence as it is lived and revealed that might not lie in the frameworks produced within institutions and dominant discourses. A more involved relationship with participants brings questions about who possesses and uses power to the fore, both relationally and structurally. The give-and-take created in any intimate relationship is powerful enough to change all of the people involved, and the researcher-participant relationship is no different. On the other hand, engaging an embodied feminist methodology gives us additional context for considering gender-based violence. Carefully tuning into where embodiment impacts how we receive knowledge allows us to also understand how we create and shape what we call truth. While it is important to name the impact of these entanglements between interlocutor and researcher, at the same time, it is vital to recognize how the internal entanglements are generative. How are we affected as researchers? As knowers and producers of knowledge? What is the impact of our embodiment and entanglements on the research? If we are attuned to it, an embodied methodology provides gender violence researchers a rich space from which to consider meaning-making and social understanding.

The authors whose work form this part of the book take up how an embodied methodological approach impacts the gender violence researcher, training their academic gaze tridirectionally toward the interlocutor's meaning/world-making, the external social and cultural world, and their own internal world simultaneously. These authors also reflect on how that shift in gaze impacts gender-based violence work broadly and the difficult choices presented to researchers when they are nested within sociopolitical spaces.

Allison Bloom's chapter 5, "From Frontline Worker to Anthropologist: Shifting My Gaze on Intimate Partner Violence," is a frank discussion about lessons learned and mistakes made grappling with ethnographic awakening in a gender-based violence agency. Bloom's reflection on her positional and perspective shift is especially relevant for applied anthropologists or anthropologists returning to study a familiar setting in an academic role. Her commitment to feminist research meant navigating past solidarities across the agency, thus differently balancing critical and empathetic "seeing" in these spaces. Witnessing the embodied realities of Latina survivors of intimate partner violence positioned as a researcher rather than as a frontline worker meant gaining perspective on previously neglected, ignored, or misunderstood dimensions of the work. As the title indicates, Bloom's experience illuminates where examining an environment, through embodied methodology, often also means examining one's own shifting gaze.

Similarly, Corinne Schwarz's aim in chapter 6, "'Can You Tell Me a Story?': Speaking Alongside Anti-Trafficking Narratives," is to think through the stories that we can tell in solidarity with victim/survivors when we speak alongside them rather than for them. Schwarz examines how frontline workers in the anti-trafficking sector use dominant narrative conventions, tropes, and discourses to voyeuristically infantilize young women. Schwarz addresses the complexities of amplifying and resisting mainstream anti-trafficking discourses, focusing on how trauma can be embedded in the listening to and retelling of victimization stories. In doing so, Schwarz notes her position "often serving as an interlocutor for interlocutors" in research where she regularly "uses stories in messy, layered ways" focusing on the tension between the ideologies and the lived realities of sexuality and labor.

In chapter 7, "What Gets Lost: At the Intersection of Gender-Based Violence and Racist Scholarship of the Arab Gulf," Hasnaa Mokhtar examines the racist stereotypes as well as micro- and macroaggressions that prevail in the canon of work on the Arab Gulf. Her frank discussion focuses on the impact of research that is ignorant of or about the history of colonization and the legacies of orientalist tropes. She draws attention to how colonial ways of producing knowledge on the Arab Gulf countries have aided and sustained state-led and religiously sanctioned structural and interpersonal violence in the region. Using a decolonial feminist lens, Mokhtar discusses her work on gender violence in Kuwait City, while centering the theoretical work of Muslim, Arab, and BIPoC scholars to highlight how scholarly literature and development-led reports might return the "lost" gendered, local realities that are otherwise silenced.

The work of thinking through power and domination, evident in the discourses and canons revealed in this part of the book, pushes the researcher to new places. Perhaps it reshapes our expectations that were reliant on false dichotomies and access to privileged, sanitized discourses in the academy. Perhaps it fractures our relationships, even as new ones are created, calling attention to changing dynamics and responsibilities. And perhaps it reframes our worldview and our participation in the hegemony of knowledge production of which we assumed we lay outside. Such questions, and the sometimes-painful answers, move the reader into part 2, where contributors address what it might mean to do research and produce knowledge for social change and justice—and to engage in methodologies that are meant to heal.

REFERENCES

Craven, Christa, and Dána-Ain Davis. 2013. *Feminist Activist Ethnography: Counterpoints to Neoliberalism in North America*. Lanham, MD: Lexington Books.

Davis, Dána-Ain. 2013. "Border Crossings: Intimacy and Feminist Activist Ethnography in the Age of Neoliberalism." In *Feminist Activist Ethnography: Counterpoints to Neoliberalism in North America*, edited by Christa Craven and Dána-Ain Davis, 23–38. Lanham, MD: Lexington Books.

Dotson, Kristie. 2011. "Tracking Epistemic Violence, Tracking Practices of Silencing." *Hypatia* 26 (2): 236–57. http://doi.org/10.1111/j.1527-2001.2011.01177.x.

Harding Sandra. 1987. *Feminism and Methodology: Social Science Issues*. Bloomington: Indiana University Press.

Hlavka, Heather R. 2019. "Regulating Bodies: Children and Sexual Violence." *Violence Against Women* 25 (6): 1956–79.

Petillo, April. 2020. "Unsettling Ourselves: Notes on Reflective Listening beyond Discomfort." *Feminist Anthropology* 1 (1): 14–23.

Stacey, Judith. 1988. "Can There Be a Feminist Ethnography?" *Women's Studies International Forum* 11 (1): 21–27.

5

From Frontline Worker to Anthropologist

Shifting My Gaze on Intimate Partner Violence

ALLISON BLOOM

"Entering" the Field

Most contemporary anthropologists will never have the proverbial experience of "entering the field" in the way we read about in our traditional anthropological training: the mythical experience of entering into a foreign land to entirely new faces and surroundings. For applied anthropologists or anthropologists studying their own communities, there may be nothing at all unfamiliar about even "new" research settings, as these are often settings in which they may already have had years of contact in various capacities. This was certainly the case for my own doctoral fieldwork, for which I returned to an intimate partner violence (IPV) crisis center where I had previously worked, located in an area where I had lived and worked for many years prior to my graduate studies.

While the setting and faces were far from new, what was new was my positionality, my role, and my training. Having this prior experience and rapport was in many ways crucial for this research on IPV, as it allowed me to have access to otherwise insular and protected spaces, given the confidential, sensitive nature of the IPV field and the typical minimum training requirements in each state in order to engage in frontline IPV services. Yet having preset expectations from the center about who I was, what I could offer, and what I was there to accomplish took some significant navigation. Ultimately, there were two distinct directions in which I found myself being pulled: my sense of obligation to my former coworkers and my responsibility to deeply investigate the lives of the survivors at the center. In my attempts to negotiate these two very different sets of relationships, I surely made mistakes, yet I ultimately learned valuable lessons about shifting one's gaze in a familiar research setting that may be helpful to others embarking on studies of gender-based violence.

Feminist scholars have long underscored the fallacy of "objective" research and promoted research that is politically motivated. For those of us who study gender-based violence, that political solidarity with survivors is fundamental to much of what we do. In many ways, this also may mean solidarity with advocates, counselors, administrators, and other frontline workers. Yet anthropology is a critical field, and we do not always paint a rosy picture of the people we study—even those with whom we may hold ourselves in political solidarity. How, then, can feminist scholars of gender-based violence manage to maintain these solidarities by being both critical and empathetic?

Moreover, when we bring an anthropological lens to a field that we saw previously as practitioners, it is part of our ethnographic aim to uncover dimensions we previously neglected, were blind to, or misunderstood. As I came to know the immigrant survivors from Latina America at this crisis center as an ethnographer, what became clear to me in a new way was the embodied dimension of violence that went far beyond the emotional and physical trauma recognized by the agency. Instead, I realized the need for moving past a crisis-centered model to one that could accommodate the long-term disabling qualities of layered violence over time—a layering effect that creates new obstacles with increasing age. In general, IPV services have limited funding, and centers must make difficult decisions about where and how to allocate their resources. As it stands, such centers are very aware of the contradictions between crisis work and the need for long-term structural reform. Yet even within their limited resources, I came to see the areas of neglect that could be better addressed with respect to age and disability, which were also realities of IPV that I had previously neglected myself. By interrogating this negotiation of my role and identity within the center as well as my shifting lens on survivor experiences, other researchers entering into work on gender-based violence—particularly those who may have existing relationships within this field—can benefit from these considerations.

Shifting Expectations

In my own case, I deliberately switched my doctoral project from an international, policy-focused study to a US-based project at an IPV crisis center that I already knew well, building on my many years of direct service experience in this field and in social services in general. I conducted a year of ethnographic research at this agency from 2015 to 2016, followed by site visits from 2016 to 2017. During that time, I focused on the center's services for Spanish-speaking survivors, a group that was made up mostly of immigrants from Central America. My hope was that this switch would provide deeper access to the more intimate spaces in which this frontline work is conducted and, ultimately, a more productive, intricate analysis of a service system to which I felt politically responsible. This also came with preset expectations on the part of the center about what I would do there and what I could provide, and created guilt on my part about not living up to these expectations.

One important expectation that I confronted was that I was there to promote these frontline workers' efforts. Certainly, I was there in solidarity with the field and sought to concretely contribute to the work wherever possible. I translated this desire into tasks like helping with day-to-day activities at the center or volunteering with fund-raising efforts. Yet reminding former colleagues that this work was, in fact, not my primary role was difficult when their needs were so great—for instance, I was often nudged to apply for open positions at the center in the hope that I would slip back into my full-time, frontline work.

Yet, as an ethnographer, I was no longer there to primarily function as a frontline worker. Moreover, I was under no obligation to uncritically amplify their specific programs in my writing or to agree with their approaches. According to the executive director—who wholeheartedly supported the project and whom I knew well from my time previously working at the center—she did desire critical feedback and understood that this was a productive part of the role I could play for the center and its efforts. However, there were many moments in which my role as a participant observer was perhaps forgotten or misunderstood or could in fact work against frontline workers who believed that I was "on their side." For instance, I would be pulled aside and told criticisms of survivors or other frontline workers that were probably not intended for inclusion in my ethnographic data. However, these precise moments of friction often made for the best ethnographic illustrations. Thus, I had to be judicious with how I would include these asides in my writing, consistently remind people of my new role, and be considerate with my criticisms of this crisis-driven work.

Another expectation was that I would adhere to the center's procedures for employees and volunteers. While on the surface, this seemed like sound practice, often these formal rules and informal guidelines were incompatible with expectations for ethnographic fieldwork. For example, it was considered best practice for frontline workers at the center not to acknowledge survivors outside the center or to interact with them in the community outside of their advocacy roles (such as at the courthouse or in other social service centers). The logic behind this practice was to promote the safety of both survivors and frontline workers by not compromising their confidentiality outside the center's spaces and by minimizing the risk of exposing anyone's work at the center to potentially angry or antagonistic third parties, particularly current or former abusive partners. Indeed, there were incidents in which survivors were told that they had to discontinue services at the center because they had compromised the identity of another survivor. In these small communities—even smaller within the particular circles of Latina survivors that I primarily worked with in this research—word spread quickly, making these precautions understandable.

However, as an ethnographer, confining my ethnographic interactions to the walls of the center's spaces was at times little understood or supported by other anthropologists who were not used to this type of institutional constraint. Eventually, I found ways to interact with survivors beyond the institution, such as accompanying them to court, visiting church services, or attending social events. Yet as a white woman speaking discernably nonnative Spanish, I have no doubt that regularly accompanying survivors out in the community would have been conspicuous. At the end of the day, supporting everyone's safety—and not compromising my relationship with the center by overstepping its boundaries—took priority over attempting more "traditional" ethnographic methods.

A New Lens on an Old Setting

Somewhat ironically, I was also discouraged from spending too much time advocating on behalf of survivors. While frontline workers at the center certainly spent a great deal of time advocating—in courthouses, with landlords, even with phone companies—there was still an underlying premise that survivors should learn to advocate for themselves and that frontline workers should not do tasks for them that they could accomplish on their own. Some of this ideology was based on the basic financial and personnel constraints of the agency and the reality that the services they could provide were short term and limited. Yet some of these constraints were also based on the goal of promoting neoliberal ideas about self-sufficiency and independence that have been critiqued for their lack of an intersectional feminist perspective (Haldane 2011; Mehrotra, Kimball, and Wahab 2016)—neoliberal notions that are also infused throughout our entire US welfare system (Adelman 2004).

It was precisely this neoliberal quality that I became most wary of while returning to this field as an anthropologist. As a frontline worker with an academic background in women's and gender studies, before my graduate training in anthropology, I was deeply entrenched in only particular Western feminist ideologies and driven by what seemed most practical from a day-to-day standpoint. It was not until I brought the lens and training of an anthropologist to this same setting that I could see the shortcomings of these neoliberal expectations.

What began to call my attention were the layers of violence that immigrant survivors from Latin America had faced—oftentimes over the course of decades, even their whole lives—and how this led to long-term disabilities and increasing embodied hardship with age. Even for middle-aged immigrant survivors, they constantly had to negotiate between their own physical and psychological needs and the needs of the families that they cared for—familial webs of responsibility in which they were deeply and complexly situated. This sense of personal sacrifice, even of one's own health well into middle and older age, was squarely incompatible with the notions of self-reliance and self-promotion taught by the center and the larger services system of which it was part. This nuanced understanding of these embodied needs, and the ways that these crisis-oriented services failed to acknowledge or accommodate many of these more subtle—although, eventually, not subtle at all—needs, was something that I was unaware of during my time as a frontline worker in this field, and it is an awareness that I often found lacking in the frontline workers at this and other service sites as well.

These insights also came at a particularly interesting moment in the United States. The US is growing undeniably older: between 2000 and 2016, the median national age rose from 35.3 years to 37.9 years. During this time, people over sixty-five grew from 12.4 percent to 15.2 percent of the total population—a 2.8 percent increase (US Census Bureau 2017). For Latinx immigrants in particular, in 2014 there were 3.6 million Latinx people aged sixty-five or older in the US, making up 8 percent of the older population. By 2060, this population is projected to nearly triple to 22 percent of the older population (ACL 2017), creating an urgent need for more understanding of this population's experiences. While IPV may be statistically most common for women between eighteen and twenty-four years of age, elder abuse is highly underreported, and family members perpetrate 76 percent of the four million cases of elderly abuse each year in the US (NCADV 2015). Among the women whom I interviewed and worked with most closely, over half were over forty, with a couple of women well into their sixties. Moreover, while the health effects of abuse are now starting to be more widely acknowledged, not nearly enough is done in the way of training health and social service professionals accordingly. This is especially true when it comes to services for Latinx and elderly survivors of IPV. This lack of attentiveness to these issues in social and health services, along with a woeful lack of infrastructure and resources for caring for the growing elderly population, is becoming increasingly problematic on a national level. The deficit in research on the intersection of immigration, violence, gender, disability, and age is also reflected in the ethnographic scholarship on gender-based violence—indeed, in the scholarship on violence in general.

What was it about this shift in positionality that allowed me to see the shortcomings of this system in a new light? And what would I do with this knowledge? First, it is important for me to acknowledge that entering into this space as an anthropologist rather than a frontline worker was a position of privilege. Frontline workers often conduct their counseling and advocacy under extremely stressful and strained conditions—

low wages, few benefits, inadequate facilities, limited resources, and long hours, to name a few. While the professionalization of this field has meant better conditions on each of these fronts, any kind of crisis-driven work is inevitably going to be a difficult type of job where workers are pulled in many different and often competing directions (Wies 2008; Haldane 2011; Kolb 2014). Frontline workers have to establish consistent boundaries in order to maintain any kind of longevity in this work (Wies 2008) and often have to function on a day-to-day, "just getting by" mentality. These are not conditions well suited to deep contemplation or larger structural change, yet somehow, advocates in this field have still made huge strides in systems-level and service-level improvement over the past few decades.

Having my time be solely devoted to ethnographic fieldwork rather than frontline work was a significant factor in my ability to analyze these services and systems so deeply. Engaging in long-term participant observation at the center, lengthy interviews with survivors, conversations across a cross-section of staff plus community partners, and deep analysis of patterns or standout moments throughout this collected data was a luxury that no frontline worker ever gets afforded. Moreover, my training as an anthropologist helped me to contemplate survivors' hardships and decisions outside of a Western feminist lens and take their own frameworks as the basis of analysis (Wies and Haldane 2011). These methodological and analytical skills both facilitated seeing these gaps in services to which I once was blind. Yet as an applied anthropologist—and in the spirit of the feminist methodologies to which I hold myself—my political solidarity made me acutely aware that I had to use these findings carefully and productively. Ultimately, my dual positionality as a former frontline worker and an anthropologist again required that I look at things through both sets of eyes, offering solutions as well as empathetic critiques of this current work.

Careful Representation

Another important piece of this dual-role puzzle was the challenge of writing and representation. It would be unethical and cavalier of me to represent the lives of the survivors with too much hyperbole or to critique the efforts of frontline workers without offering any concrete solutions. Writing about the everyday interactions between these two groups of people would require careful attention and understanding of their different intentions, constraints, and needs. While as an academic I care about theoretical contributions, rarely does theory do people and their everyday lives much direct good. Moreover, part of the task of doing politically engaged work is to formulate and disseminate more practical findings across a variety of platforms: for other scholars, yes, but also for practitioners and for the public.

With respect to public scholarship, for researchers such as myself who work on issues like gender-based violence and immigration, spreading the word about our insights takes on a political importance that goes beyond a sense of obligation to get outside the ivory tower. Instead, the stakes for the people with whom I work can in many cases be a matter of health and well-being, potentially even life or death. As a graduate student, much of my work remained confined to the walls of my educational institution and the occasional scholarly space like a conference. Yet as my scholarship and I transitioned from this more insular world to wider public audiences, the spaces and manner in which I represented this scholarship became a constant weight on my mind.

As Arthur Kleinman (1997) pointed out over twenty years ago now, graphic images and representations of violence have been used in the media to wield state control: a warning to citizens of what can happen should they step out of line. Moreover, a *lack* of media representation can be used to deny the realities of everyday violence and assert an idealized imagery of citizen life. Both serve to create "cultures of fear" (Kleinman 1997, 175) by which repressive governments can reinforce their agendas through modes of representation and instill further helplessness and mistrust. As Kleinman summarizes, "trauma is used systematically to silence people through suffering" (175). Kleinman further points to another facet of representation that is equally troubling. As he notes, "When those who experience violence escape to places of refuge, they must submit to yet another type of violation. Their memories of violation, their *trauma stories* become the currency with which they enter exchanges for physical resources" (176). Here we see reverberations of earlier arguments made by feminist scholars and scholars from communities of color around the politics of representation. Following this earlier tradition, anthropologists of gender, violence, and humanitarianism continue to question this moral economy of victimhood and violence within justice systems, international NGOs, and other hierarchical spaces. Scholars such as Sally Engle Merry (2006), Madelaine Adelman (2017), Nia Parson (2013), and Miriam Ticktin (2011) have written extensively around how people seeking claims within human rights and social service systems—particularly women—not only must prove their innocence, but must prove their *exceptional* victimhood. Their narratives must reflect suffering that goes beyond everyday violence: that alone does not make one worthy of consideration on a geopolitical stage.

Yet in today's world of social and streaming media, the nature of this messaging around violence has taken on somewhat of a more dialectic quality. Social media is both a tool and a weapon. It can be used to disseminate messages to the masses by any layperson with internet access while simultaneously reifying the potentially damaging and damning messages by those in power whom Kleinman earlier described. However, as we continue to become more and more socially aware, these spaces are far from neutral. The mechanisms behind these virtual worlds are deeply embedded in the power of market economies and can be easily corrupted by political regimes. Additionally, what we put out into this virtual space takes on a life of its own and can be taken up and used in a multitude of ways unintended by its original author.

How, then, do engaged and applied scholars keep up with this politics of representation? In a sea of messages where traditional scholarly "expertise" is easily dismissed—and where everyone is encouraged to assert their opinion as equally valid, no matter how fabricated or uninformed—how do we represent our scholarship in ways that are attention-grabbing and convincing without exploiting or sensationalizing the experiences of our interlocutors? How do we amplify those voices without overshadowing them with our own?

While these questions are far from new, perhaps what has changed through the advent of social media is the speed at which we have to constantly negotiate and renegotiate this representation of our work, the modes through which we must do so, the constant interactions between users and streaming media, and the sheer volume of opinions and information that are now available at a moment's glance. How does one represent one's work in sensitive, critical, engaged, yet attention-grabbing ways when limited to 280 characters? How can one garner attention for one's work without exploitative sensationalizing when the mainstream media and the rest of social media users are held to a different standard? The "click-bait" culture of the current media climate virtually requires that one's titles, images, and openers be sensationalized, or they will easily get passed over in the extreme volume of other messages. These issues make it necessary for us to have new conversations around these older themes and not take for granted that the old cautions will hold out against these shifting realities.

Choosing Words, Choosing Platforms

In my efforts to avoid exploiting my interlocutors' voices, I have tried to balance my own voice against those of survivors in particular ways. I tend to start off pieces of writing with ethnographic vignettes that highlight the perspectives of a person relevant to that topic. While, of course, these narratives are inevitably mediated through my own thoughts and written construction, by foregrounding insights that survivors were adamant about reinforcing, I hope to at least, in my own small way, provide a platform for their thoughts and ideas and assert them front and center. Yet many of the stories I was told during my fieldwork and throughout my time in social services were quite graphic and disturbing and could lend themselves to the trap of sensationalized use. In this sense, the inevitable "craftedness" of ethnographic writing is not such a bad thing: I am able to make my own decisions as an author about which insights I ought to foreground and how to do so in politically and ethically strategic ways. While the more shocking stories would be attention-grabbing, they were not necessarily the insights most representative of larger patterns in my research, and using them just to engage an audience could be unnecessarily exploitative. Instead, I choose vignettes that are engaging yet most representative of the particular topic at hand.

With regard to choosing platforms, as I share my findings more and more publicly, being in conversation with practitioners, "think tanks," and other more applied researchers has been of the utmost importance. My Twitter account is dedicated to following institutions and individuals directly working on related issues and engaging in their advocacy and education efforts as part of a larger public conversation. Mainly, I use this type of space to circulate training opportunities and relevant news articles that confirm and address the issues related to my applied research, as well as to comment and converse in relevant exchanges. While platforms such as Twitter determine the scope of any particular engagement, the audience must, of course, as well. One strategy I have begun to try has been addressing the same issue from different angles—targeting different audiences—across multiple platforms and then linking these pieces together. For example, I posted a blog around mental health in immigrant communities for *Medical Anthropology Quarterly* (Bloom 2017b) and linked that blog post to a sister post around ethical and methodological considerations for graduate students interested in conducting ethnography around mental health and immigration on the *Medical Anthropology Student Association Blog* (Bloom 2017a). In so doing, I had to flex my muscles pedagogically and with regard to writing to gain more traction for certain issues in ways that were relevant for particular audiences. With respect to policy, I have begun to engage the aspects most relevant to my findings and to intervene where I think I could contribute a helpful insight. For example, in a piece for *Anthropology News*, I wrote about the legislative efforts to repeal and replace the Affordable Care Act, discussing why this would be devastating to many survivors of IPV from the perspective of violence and aging (Bloom 2018).

In addition to public platforms and scholarly works, I have also aimed to engage practitioners more directly. The reality is that very few frontline IPV workers have access to scholarly journals or the time to sift through theoretical jargon to get to any practical insights (if there even are any!). Borrowing from the field of social work, developing publicly available and directly applicable "practitioner toolkits" to accompany major scholarly interventions has become an aim of mine, in the hope of making these findings accessible and usable by frontline workers and their institutions. Additionally, writing up more directly applicable findings into research briefs—which can then be used for grant applications, funder reports, trainings, and so on—for the centers where I conduct my research is another way that I can live up to their expectations for solidarity and contribute to this work as someone with intimate frontline knowledge. In all my writing, I am careful to acknowledge frontline workers' working constraints while being critical of the need for growth in certain areas. While people may be wary of having a mirror held up to themselves, often frontline workers are also very aware of certain flaws in their own work. Therefore, offering practical and implementable solutions has become one of the most productive ways that I have been able to connect with frontline workers through these critiques.

As a former frontline worker, it is my hope that being able to still engage with practitioners and advocates in relevant ways through my lens as an anthropologist will help anthropology remain relevant to these spaces and conversations, rather than just reverberating back on itself. At the same time, I continue to heed the warnings of feminist scholars and scholars of color around the politics of representation, particularly in light of the rising stakes for my work and the twists and turns of the ever-changing worlds of social welfare and social media. While negotiating across different political solidarities within a field site is challenging, I have found that it can also be one of the most fruitful and rewarding ways that feminist anthropology can contribute to the field of gender-based violence.

REFERENCES

Adelman, Madelaine. 2004. "The Battering State: Towards a Political Economy of Domestic Violence." *Journal of Poverty* 8 (3): 45–64.

———. 2017. *Battering States: The Politics of Domestic Violence in Israel.* Nashville, TN: Vanderbilt University Press.

ACL (Administration for Community Living). 2017. "Minority Aging." Last modified September 5, 2017. www.acl.gov.

Bloom, Allison. 2017a. "Methodology and Mental Health: A Guide for Graduate Students." *Medical Anthropology Student Association Blog*, October 2017. http://masa. medanthro.net.

———. 2017b. "The Stakes for Immigration and Mental Health." *Critical Care: Medical Anthropology Quarterly*, August 2017. http://medanthroquarterly.org.

———. 2018. "When Short-Term Care Isn't Enough: Maturing Survivors of Domestic Violence Need a Long-Term Life Course Approach to Health Care." *Anthropology News* (American Anthropological Association), January 2018. https://anthrosource. onlinelibrary.wiley.com.

Haldane, Hillary. 2011. "Motivation Matters: Shelter Workers and Residents in the Late Capitalist Era." *Practicing Anthropology* 33 (3): 9–12.

Kleinman, Arthur. 1997. "Violence, Culture, and the Politics of Trauma." In *Writing at the Margin: Discourse between Anthropology and Medicine*, 173–89. Berkeley: University of California Press.

Kolb, Kenneth H. 2014. *Moral Wages.* Oakland: University of California Press.

Mehrotra, Gita R., Ericka Kimball, and Stephanie Wahab. 2016. "The Braid That Binds Us: The Impact of Neoliberalism, Criminalization, and Professionalization on Domestic Violence Work." *Affilia* 31 (2): 153–63.

Merry, Sally Engle. 2006. *Human Rights and Gender Violence: Translating International Law into Local Justice.* Chicago: University of Chicago Press.

NCADV (National Coalition Against Domestic Violence). 2015. "Statistics: National Statistics." https://ncadv.org.

Parson, Nia. 2013. *Traumatic States: Gendered Violence, Suffering, and Care in Chile.* Nashville, TN: Vanderbilt University Press.

Ticktin, Miriam Iris. 2011. *Casualties of Care: Immigration and the Politics of Humanitarianism in France.* Berkeley: University of California Press.

US Census Bureau. 2017. "The Nation's Older Population Is Still Growing, Census Bureau Reports." Newsroom, June 22, 2017. www.census.gov.

Wies, Jennifer R. 2008. "Professionalizing Human Services: A Case of Domestic Violence Shelter Advocates." *Human Organization* 67 (2): 221–33.

Wies, Jennifer R., and Hillary J. Haldane. 2011. "Ethnographic Notes from the Front Lines of Gender-Based Violence." In *Anthropology at the Front Lines of Gender-Based Violence,* edited by Jennifer R. Wies and Hillary J. Haldane, 1–18. Nashville, TN: Vanderbilt University Press.

6

"Can You Tell Me a Story?"

Speaking Alongside Anti-Trafficking Narratives

CORINNE SCHWARZ

I am sitting in a small, fluorescent-lit office, balancing my notebook and audio recorder on my lap to avoid adding to the clutter and paper on the lawyer's desk. Or maybe I am one of seven people sitting in folding chairs in a large, gymnasium-like space in a nonprofit complex, quietly navigating the interpersonal dimensions of a group interview. Perhaps I am with a law enforcement officer in a room primarily used for interrogations, the only quiet space for us to conduct our interview in the suburban jail facility. Regardless, it is the end of our time together—we have been talking for twenty-five minutes, an hour, sometimes longer—and I am approaching the end of my interview protocol, the list of questions approved by the institutional review board that I have prepared to guide our conversation on human trafficking in the midwestern US.

I ask the final formal question on this piece of paper: "Can you tell me a story about a case, a client, a situation, an experience that you would consider successful, in however you define 'success'? What about an example that would be considered unsuccessful, in however you define that?" Sometimes my participants waver, demurring that they are not a good storyteller. "That's okay," I reassure. "I always like hearing stories and anecdotes." Others return to an example mentioned in passing earlier in our interview, expanding on a young Central American woman returning to her family or a formerly incarcerated sex worker navigating parole and its restrictions. A few reject the premise outright, like one law enforcement officer who attempted to qualify the unsuccessful moments in his work: "Gosh, I can't say. I don't like the word 'failure' because I used to coach" (interview 8/10/16).

In my research, I am broadly interested in how frontline workers—those who directly encounter vulnerable, exploited, or trafficked clients in their day-to-day practices—make sense of their role in broader anti-sex- and labor-trafficking efforts.[1] What anti-trafficking policies, organizational mandates, or informal practices do they mobilize in their encounters with clients? How do they talk about their clients in ways that resist or support the "master narrative" (Hill 2016) of human trafficking? Where do they fall in the "detention-to-protection" pipeline (Musto 2013) that embeds trafficked persons in larger carceral mechanisms?

To answer these questions, I have deliberately chosen to interview service providers, not trafficked persons themselves, though I would be remiss to see these as two completely different populations. As with other sectors that address gender-based violence, some frontline workers come to these workplaces *because of* their experiences with trauma, exploitation, or trafficking. The complexity of our lived experiences means that some survivors of sex or labor trafficking will eventually become the service providers disseminating resources. At the same time, not all of my interviewees operate with the same baseline expertise or understanding of human trafficking's violence and exploitation. Some compare human trafficking to plotlines in TV melodramas and action films; others offer definitions that have no legal grounding, like describing human trafficking as a phenomenon that can only happen to undocumented migrants or that must require some kind of interstate or transnational movement. In short, the stories I get about human trafficking are complicated, contradictory, and charged with a variety of competing emotions.

In this chapter, I attempt to work through the complexities of storytelling in qualitative, antiviolence scholarship. My own research uses stories in messy, layered ways. Because I am interviewing service providers about their practices of doing the *work* of anti-trafficking work—and because the majority of my participants do not self-identify as survivors in our interviews—I am often serving as an interlocutor for interlocutors. I receive stories, some of which use particularly troubling tropes that reaffirm certain isms and phobias, and translate them into academic work informed by my own orientation toward critical trafficking studies and anticarceral feminisms. This can be profoundly uncomfortable work, especially when participants' processes of "speaking for themselves" (itself a notion to be problematized [Mazzei and Jackson 2012]) are mismatched with my own theoretical and political commitments.

The sections that follow offer some clarity on what continues to be an affectively potent, opaque process for me. I begin by introducing the larger terrain of anti-trafficking narratives and storytelling, specifically focusing on the tension between particular ideologies of sexuality and labor. I then move toward Linda Alcoff's (1991) "speaking for" others and Sara Ahmed's (2017) feminist killjoy, two theories that continually swirl in my head as I conduct interviews and analyze qualitative data. Next, I offer some illustrative examples of how these moments of discomfort and mismatch emerged in interviews I conducted with anti-trafficking service providers in the midwestern US. Finally, I conclude by sharing how I have worked through these moments of complicity, guilt, and anger—knowing that these practices are partial, ever evolving, and contextual.

Telling Anti-Trafficking Stories

In a 2015 series of posts critiquing the effects of Human Trafficking Awareness Day, the prominent sex workers' rights activist Carol Leigh used the phrase "anti-trafficking industrial complex" to describe the well-funded awareness campaigns, celebrity endorsements, law enforcement operations, and trafficking-specific organizations that essentially funnel those who are marked as trafficked persons into larger systems of carceral or therapeutic control. Knowing that the quantifiable data on trafficking is messy at best (Gallagher 2017; Merry 2016), the anti-trafficking industrial complex often runs on *discourses*, the stories told and retold to fuel outrage, generate funds, or garner support. Even when these stories are proven dubious, as seen with the rise and fall of the Cambodian anti-trafficking activist Somaly Mam (Agustín 2014; Hoefinger 2016) and the QAnon-fueled conspiracy theories surrounding the online retailer Wayfair (Grant 2020), they are often still applauded for generating an understanding of trafficking's existence. Even if flawed or fundamentally inaccurate, this awareness is an uncritical victory. The material consequences of these stories on the lives of trafficked persons, sex workers, and migrant laborers—sometimes overlapping categories, sometimes more distinct—are rarely acknowledged (Busza 2006; Kinney 2006).

Within this context, there remains a powerful tension between the increased calls for "survivor-centered" trafficking narratives *and* the on-going perpetuation of anti-trafficking stereotypes and sensationalism. The desire to learn more about the "realities" of trafficking runs into the well-worn tropes of passive victimhood (Srikantiah 2007) and extreme forms of degradation, essentially "gothic portrayals of . . . (sexual) slav-ery" (Chapkis 2003, 930). To add to the complications of this tension, some of the most prominently recognized survivor-led anti-trafficking organizations in the United States use a neoabolitionist lens that sees all commercial sex as trafficking in need of carceral or social service inter-ventions.[2] In a white paper from the anti-trafficking coalition Freedom Network USA, the persistence of "social and political differences regard-ing prostitution" do impact the terrain of survivor-led anti-trafficking work: "Survivor advocates involved in leadership cultivation cite an ethi-cal and moral divide among survivors on the sex trade and approaches to address sex trafficking" (Smith 2018, 8). As well, this divide may also contribute to the limited understandings of human trafficking beyond sex trafficking; specifically, the experiences of labor-trafficking survivors or survivors whose identities are not represented by white, cisgender women with former involvement in commercial sex may be foreclosed from broader understandings of trafficking.

This dynamic culminates in secondary exploitation, "a toxic cli-mate . . . in which various actors perpetuate misleading and dehu-manising stereotypes, which contribute to the stigmatisation and marginalisation of sex workers and trafficked individuals" (Cojocaru 2016, 12). This is the context in which we are doing—and have been doing—anti-trafficking work. Survivors are compelled to retrofit their experiences into the dominant narrative of exploitation, "the powerless-ness, the shocking details, the humiliation, the horror and the sexual domination, . . . a Freak Show" (Cojocaru 2015, 187), often to gain access to meaningful resources like visas, secure shelter, and economic sup-ports, while frontline workers offer these services and resources to their clients with an idealized, stereotypical victim in mind. The necessity of the storytelling is not questioned; the relationship between formerly trafficked persons *telling* their story and service providers *retelling* it (to craft a compelling narrative for a visa application, to secure one of a few beds in a trafficking-specific shelter) is crystallized.

Who "Speaks For" Trafficked Persons?

Because of my focus on those who work with trafficked persons, not necessarily those who primarily self-identify as survivors, my research grapples with larger ethical concerns of speaking with/for/to/about others. I am reminded of my first graduate seminar in feminist theory, where we were introduced to Alcoff's "The Problem of Speaking for Others" (1991). As she writes, in the act of speaking for or about a group of which I am not a member, "I am engaging in the act of representing the other's needs, goals, situation, and in fact, *who they are*. I am representing them as such and such, or in post-structuralist terms, I am participating in the construction of their subject-positions" (9). Trafficked persons occupy a subject-position—which may not reflect their own feelings about the harms they faced or the authenticity of their own lived experiences—through the interpellation of their experiences from this mediator or observer, who is *also* becoming a subject through a similar process of framing (or even revision).

Speaking is not neutral; there are real, material effects in the telling and retelling of these stories of trafficking, exploitation, and trauma. Thinking about frontline workers creating policy on the ground, a secondhand narrative about one survivor's perceived or assumed response to an intervention—gratitude for her saviors in law enforcement, compliance under the threat of deportation—can easily morph into organizational "best practices." Alcoff also names this power: "Even if someone never hears the discursive self I present of them they may be affected by the decisions others make after hearing it" (1991, 10).

I recognize that I too am playing into these dynamics of speaking and naming, representing and foreclosing. I ask my interview participants to speak with/for/to/about the trafficked persons they have encountered, and then I speak with/for/to/about their answers to occupy the subject-position of researcher. And indeed, particularly in the early stages of this work, I attempted to minimize my own role in this telling and retelling, taking my participants' words at face value and feeling anxiety or guilt when questioning their framings of exploitation and trafficking. This affective response felt especially fraught when my interviewees conflated all forms of sex work, from stripping to pornography to street-based commercial sex, with sex trafficking or presented examples of law-enforcement-centered anti-trafficking interventions without addressing the inherent harms of the carceral state. These responses reflect ideological commitments to particular ways of speaking about trafficking with which I fundamentally disagree—even if these are arguably the more mainstream ways that human trafficking is spoken about currently in the US.

Considering this ideological tension, I try to speak as a killjoy (Ahmed 2017) when discussing or framing my findings. I try to problematize these discourses and images of victimhood as ethically and thoughtfully as possible, as a way to perhaps undo the harm of this initial speaking into being without erasing those whose experiences align more closely with iconic victimhood. As Ahmed writes, "When you expose a problem you pose a problem" (2017, 37). Here, the problem is the social construction of trafficked persons and the erasure of particular forms of violence. Ahmed continues further: "If the feminist killjoy comes up in a conversation over the table, she brings other things into view" (40). These critiques bring into view the larger, systemic violence of various isms and phobias that create material consequences for marginalized, exploited, and objectified groups.

At the same time, I still hesitate to assert this stance (to be this killjoy) in intimate, interpersonal interviewing moments. I am asking people to share their experiences with and perceptions of human trafficking, so who am I to call their bluff? And is it even calling their bluff if the experiences they share simply conform to the master narrative (Hill 2016) of trafficking? I think here of Ian Shaw's articulation of qualitative research's ethical complications: "Ethical issues are raised by the fact that as we encourage people to tell their stories, we become characters in those stories, and thus change those stories" (2008, 408). As someone ostensibly speaking for those who speak for trafficked persons, I am dealing with layers of storytelling revisions and reinterpretations.

In the next two sections, I engage in my own telling and retelling, offering some illustrative examples—think of these as genres of storytelling— that emerged across my interviews. I show how I spoke alongside my interviewees in a more critical position, in a stance that exposes and poses the problems of the dominant narrative of human trafficking.

The "Stranger Danger" of Human Trafficking

Though scholarship primed me to see examples of Wendy Chapkis's (2003) gothic narratives everywhere, it was rare for my interviewees to be so blunt in their descriptions of violence or captivity. More commonly, my interviewees mobilized a "stranger danger"–esque narrative that emphasized education to empower self-guided strategies of surveillance and vigilance. In this manner of storytelling, the victimized subject was introduced as a naïve figure whose innocence prevented them from seeing a seedy, exploitative reality. For example, when asked about the unique challenges of trafficked clients in a more rural part of the Midwest, a crisis pregnancy center (CPC) director described a bait-and-switch from fake modeling scams to grooming to eventual (potentially coercive) sex work: "It's the girl that's being asked at Walmart to sign a modeling contract 'cause she's so awesome and amazing and beautiful, and it starts with such a grooming process. And so, by the time I get her, she's probably eighteen and a half, nineteen, and now she's doing porn" (interview 6/1/17). Though this may feel extreme, a genre of religious anti-trafficking activism does conflate sex trafficking with forms of regulated commercial sex, like pornography and stripping.[3] In this CPC director's retelling of this story, she invokes the voyeuristic tropes of a fall from grace, or "the rigid limitations of melodrama" (Vance 2011, 205), the ingenue's beauty being degraded and cheapened.

A state-level government employee focused on the vulnerability of youth using social media and engaging with strangers in public spaces, specifically naming catfishing schemes on Facebook and unknown people trying to talk to teenagers at local department stores as potential sites of exploitation. She identified continued education on the signs of human trafficking, especially for "good kids," coded language that she then extrapolated to mean middle-class teens who "might not be vigilant." While there are a host of problematic assumptions here—namely, that goodness and worth are equated with race and class, creating an almost inevitable harm for those youths operating outside of white, middle-class respectability—I want to focus on how this government employee used the figure of the stranger in her framing of trafficking. As opposed to robust empirical scholarship that identifies the harms of trafficking in global economic policies that perpetuate structural inequalities (Kempadoo 2015) or complicates the figure of the trafficker as a friend or family member (Marcus et al. 2014), she uses the most affectively potent tropes left over from the white-slave panics at the turn of the twentieth century: "a young and naive innocent lured or deceived by evil traffickers into a life of sordid horror from which escape is nearly impossible" (Doezema 1999, 24).

Across both of these interviews, I distinctly remember my own discomfort as these participants used this "stranger danger" framework to describe their work. My gut impulse was to take these tales in "bad faith," specifically for their mobilization of anti-sex-work keywords and thinly veiled racism and classism. And in the moment, I certainly did not push back on their empirically dubious claims, as there certainly are cases that resemble the dominant narratives of trafficking, problematic assumptions and all. With distance, I have tried to revisit their words more generously, asking myself if there is a way to reconcile the ways they describe trafficking without rationalizing away the stigmas and stereotypes they promote. Even if trafficking, in their communities, does fit a "stranger danger" framework, there are definitely practical concerns to address: how education is targeted only to certain populations of "at-risk" individuals, how race and class operate fatalistically in determining who is "more likely" to be exploited, how labor trafficking is absent from the conversation even though labor exploitation still exists in environments deemed the exclusive purview of commercial sex.

Telling and Retelling of Traumas

Though the majority of my interviews were professional, almost formal, they were not fully devoid of emotion or affective responses. These responses were fully understandable; as one foster-care administrator succinctly explained, "When you're dealing with victims of human trafficking, the things that you already see and hear in child welfare can be disturbing enough. But then you add human trafficking on top of that, it's just another layer" (interview 11/17/16). Expressions of sadness and disappointment were common. On rare occasions, my interviewees cried, as one youth services worker in the homelessness sector did while sharing a particularly fraught client story:

So I'll specifically talk about one youth, and I have permission to talk about her story. She has been with us since she was seventeen. . . . Her mom said she didn't want to deal with her anymore. . . . She was getting to be too much for her, she couldn't handle her. . . . And it's a horrible story, but I won't get too much into it. But her mother married this man, and they all got family name tattoos, even her, and then she was raped about a month later by him. . . . And oh, it's such a horrible story. It's one of the only ones that makes me emotional. [*Crying*] Because I don't get emotional very often. I'm sorry. . . . She's like, "I'm too stupid to graduate. I'm too stupid to get a job." And these were not her words. These are words that someone fed her her whole life, and so we just really worked on relationship building with her. . . . I was her case manager when she first came on, which is why I'm so emotionally involved with her. (Interview 12/7/16)

I felt a sense of empathy in this moment and felt myself tearing up as well. In another interview with a youth services worker, this one in the anti-sexual-violence sector, I distinctly recall the bittersweet description of "goody bags" that her organization would give to children after forensic interviews, in which they had to explain the trauma and harm they had faced: "It's just junk, you know. You go to Dollar General and go crazy. . . . And they're just going, 'Oh my gosh,' and they walk away with a silly little bag that has made their day. And it is so sad, but yet that's our reward" (interview 8/4/16).

Similar to Hannah Britton's (2020) interviews with service providers in South African gender-based violence work, some of whom saw themselves as more likely to experience the harms their clients faced, a few of my interviewees described how this awareness of some of the worst forms of violence and harm led them to see trafficking everywhere. One foster-care administrator described how a screening of *Nefarious*, a religiously produced documentary about commercial sex, served as an "eye-opening experience" for her own understanding of human trafficking in her community: "It began to open my eyes to this world of anti-trafficking, and when I started doing research about it here in [my city], the amount of massage parlors that are here is astronomical. I mean, it was baffling, and I was so angry" (interview 5/24/17). This administrator went so far as to take her identified "at-risk" youths to particular spaces in town that she associated with commercial sex, like the afore-mentioned massage parlors and corners associated with street-based sex work.

This was a more difficult emotional moment for me to navigate because it crossed into the feelings of mismatch I noted when navigating "stranger danger" tropes. *Nefarious* is not "neutral" about human trafficking in Cambodia and Thailand; its director and producer, Benjamin Nolot, is the CEO of Exodus Cry, an evangelical organization with anti-abortion and anti-LGBTQ+ doctrines alongside its anti-trafficking, neoabolitionist mission (Provost and Whyte 2018). The film also decontextualizes trafficking from larger structural factors, such as poverty and global capitalism, thus collapsing "the issue of sex trafficking . . . under the melodrama, utilizing the binaristic conventions of dramatic narrative—good versus evil—which neglect the circumstances in which trafficking occurs" (Stiles 2018, 41). Trafficking becomes a free-floating signifier that can be placed onto anything, including this foster-care administrator's midwestern community, but this decontextualization fails to account for the unique factors that may shape how youth in this region experience precarity and vulnerability. Again, trafficking *can* look like *Nefarious*, but it is far more likely to look like something else, something less easily dramatized: for example, a youth in foster care bouncing from couch to couch after aging out of programming, trading sex to maintain some kind of locational stability.

In my own experiences, I rarely metabolized these stories into sadness or fear. My primary emotion during my fieldwork was anger—anger at the systems and structures that perpetuated poverty and stigma, which I identified as major drivers of exploitation, *and* anger that the criminal justice system still seemed to be the only place where frontline workers could situate their anti-trafficking efforts. When describing my research to others, regardless of their place inside or beyond academia, they often expressed surprise that I did not feel retraumatized myself. After hearing all the ways people speak with/for/to/about trafficking, it was only reasonable to assume that I was broken down by the incessant descriptions of fraud, force, or coercion, right?

I think of how Audre Lorde talks about anger: "But anger expressed and translated into action in the service of our vision and our future is a liberating and strengthening act of clarification. . . . Anger is loaded with information and energy" (1984, 127). If anger does not metastasize into impotent guilt, it can be the catalyst for sometimes difficult, often uncomfortable, yet still necessary connection and growth. My anger carries with it a feeling of momentum and potential. Instead of feeling guilt for sharing my research, which I often liken to bursting the bubble of antitrafficking awareness previously held by the recipient of this knowledge, can I instead think about the energy transference between me and these scholarly or activist peer networks? There is useful potential in illuminating my own rage—about the ramifications of capitalism or xenophobia or carceral injustice on the experiences of individual people—if that anger can move us to a collective place of agitating against these larger systems of violence and harm.

In the face of resisting sensationalism, I often find myself becoming cynical. Does anything I publish in an academic journal or critique with my students matter when we still see anti-trafficking pseudoscience on the front page of local newspapers on the eve of the Super Bowl, promising record numbers of arrests that will nearly exclusively ensnare sex workers in further carceral surveillance and punishment? Or when viral Facebook posts warn observant mothers that their children are at risk of trafficking in Ikea parking lots? I sometimes feel like I am swimming against the current of popular human-trafficking stories that carry more resonance than the critiques of global capitalism, white supremacy, and gender- and sexuality-based stigmas.

But then I remember that I am angry. And this anger can be the way to move from guilt and stagnation to radical, social change. I conclude here not with the solutions to my anger, because I am still trying to determine what those solutions look like, but with the questions I return to in my moments of exasperation, when my passion for eradicating violence and exploitation slightly dims under the onslaught of stereotypical trafficking narratives. How can we, as scholars invested in the most ethical ways to produce knowledge in historically extractive systems of research, balance the emotionally charged narratives we receive with the impulse to critique their more exploitative elements? Is our critical retelling of these stories of violence perpetuating the impulse to traffic in the most brutal depictions of gender-based violence or downplaying the real trauma faced by unknown survivors? What stories can we tell in solidarity with—not speaking for but speaking *alongside*—populations made vulnerable by exploitative labor, economic precarity, restrictive migration policies, and carceral mechanisms?

My speaking alongside frequently takes the form of advocating for prevention: building a more robust social welfare state that can attend to the precarity induced by the isms and phobias that shape exploitation and trafficking. Prevention is a discursive space for uniting what Elizabeth Bernstein (2010) calls the "strange bedfellows" of anti-trafficking stakeholders across political, religious, and social justice terrains. This is a bargain I have made with myself: if I am going to retell stories of trafficking that I find ideologically incompatible with my own commitments, I am going to balance this with a fierce, firm, unyielding commitment to radical, structural changes. Even if the frontline workers with whom I engage do not explicitly attend to prevention in our interviews, it implicitly bubbles up. Unprompted, I have heard law enforcement officers bemoan the defunding of state-level child protective services and foster-care case managers rail against education cuts. Across political registration and anti-trafficking ideologies, they can come together in asking for more resources to buffer against precarity.

And yet prevention is still incomplete, as the robust social welfare state I want to see carries its own histories of social control and punishment. I cannot ignore the anti-Blackness of child welfare programs (Roberts 2002) or the compounding racism and classism of poverty governance embedded in welfare case management (Soss, Fording, and Schram 2011). But I would rather choose the "enemy" of the social welfare state than the carceral state. I would rather speak alongside those advocates and scholars reckoning with the illusion of the "helping" hand of state than granting any further authority or cover to the "punishing" hand of the prison nation.

NOTES

1. As a note on language, I use "trafficked person," "client," "victim," and "survivor" interchangeably throughout this chapter. This is not to prioritize one framing over another but rather to reflect the varied ways people talk about their experiences and the experiences of others facing trauma, harm, and trafficking.
2. Compounding this even further, as if the terrain of anti-trafficking efforts could not be more complicated, this exclusive focus on sexual exploitation is not reflected in survivor-led policy endeavors. For example, the National Survivors Network (NSN), one of the longest-running survivor-led networks in the United

States, offered a three-pronged policy agenda for the 2019–20 legislative year; all of the prioritized policies focused on increasing wages and improving protections for migrant laborers and reducing the long-term consequences of criminal records for formerly trafficked persons. There is no reference to the "End Demand"–style policies that criminalize the purchase of commercial sex that have become synonymous with neoabolitionism.

3. For more on this, see the recent press that Exodus Cry launched after the 2020 Super Bowl halftime show (Phillips 2020) or Fight the New Drug's (2017) consistent messaging that pornography *is* human trafficking because of a lack of consent. It would be remiss of me not to mention that these are empirically dubious claims (Weitzer 2007).

REFERENCES

Agustín, Laura. 2014. "Somaly Mam, Nick Kristof, and the Cult of Personality." *Jacobin*, June 16, 2014. www.jacobinmag.com.

Ahmed, Sara. 2017. *Living a Feminist Life*. Durham, NC: Duke University Press.

Alcoff, Linda. 1991. "The Problem of Speaking for Others." *Cultural Critique* 20:5–32.

Bernstein, Elizabeth. 2010. "Militarized Humanitarianism Meets Carceral Feminism: The Politics of Sex, Rights, and Freedom in Contemporary Antitrafficking Campaigns." *Signs: Journal of Women in Culture and Society* 36 (1): 45–71.

Britton, Hannah E. 2020. *Ending Gender-Based Violence Justice and Community in South Africa*. Urbana: University of Illinois Press.

Busza, Joanna. 2006. "Having the Rug Pulled from Under Your Feet: One Project's Experience of the US Policy Reversal on Sex Work." *Health Policy and Planning* 21 (4): 329–32.

Chapkis, Wendy. 2003. "Trafficking, Migration, and the Law: Protecting Innocents, Punishing Immigrants." *Gender & Society* 17 (6): 923–37.

Cojocaru, Claudia. 2015. "Sex Trafficking, Captivity, and Narrative: Constructing Victimhood with the Goal of Salvation." *Dialectical Anthropology* 39 (2): 183–94.

———. 2016. "My Experience Is Mine to Tell: Challenging the Abolitionist Victimhood Framework." *Anti-Trafficking Review* 7:12–38.

Doezema, Jo. 1999. "Loose Women or Lost Women? The Re-emergence of the Myth of White Slavery in Contemporary Discourses of Trafficking in Women." *Gender Issues* 18 (1): 23–50.

Fight the New Drug. 2017. "How Porn Fuels Sex Trafficking." August 23, 2017. https://fightthenewdrug.org.

Gallagher, Anne T. 2017. "What's Wrong with the Global Slavery Index?" *Anti-Trafficking Review* 8:90–112.

Grant, Melissa Gira. 2020. "The Dark Obsessions of QAnon Are Merging with Mainstream Conservatism." *New Republic*, July 14, 2020. https://newrepublic.com.

Hill, Annie. 2016. "How to Stage a Raid: Police, Media and the Master Narrative of Trafficking." *Anti-Trafficking Review* 7:39–55.

Hoefinger, Heidi. 2016. "Neoliberal Sexual Humanitarianism and Story-Telling: The Case of Somaly Mam." *Anti-Trafficking Review* 7:56–78.

Kempadoo, Kamala. 2015. "The Modern-Day White (Wo)Man's Burden: Trends in Anti-trafficking and Anti-slavery Campaigns." *Journal of Human Trafficking* 1 (1): 8–20.

Kinney, Edith C. 2006. "Appropriations for the Abolitionists: Undermining Effects of the U.S. Mandatory Anti-prostitution Pledge in the Fight against Human Trafficking and HIV/AIDS." *Berkley Journal of Gender, Law & Justice* 21:158–94.

Leigh, Carol. 2015. "Anti-Trafficking Industrial Complex Awareness Month." 2nd ed. Yale University. https://glc.yale.edu.

Lorde, Audre. 1984. "The Uses of Anger." In *Sister Outsider*, 124–33. Berkeley, CA: Crossing.

Marcus, Anthony, Amber Horning, Ric Curtis, Jo Sanson, and Efram Thompson. 2014. "Conflict and Agency among Sex Workers and Pimps: A Closer Look at Domestic Minor Sex Trafficking." *Annals of the American Academy of Political and Social Science* 653 (1): 225–46.

Mazzei, Lisa A., and Alecia Y. Jackson. 2012. "Complicating Voice in a Refusal to 'Let Participants Speak for Themselves.'" *Qualitative Inquiry* 18 (9): 745–51.

Merry, Sally Engle. 2016. *The Seductions of Quantification: Measuring Human Rights, Gender Violence, and Sex Trafficking*. Chicago: University of Chicago Press.

Musto, Jennifer. 2013. "Domestic Minor Sex Trafficking and the Detention-to-Protection Pipeline." *Dialectical Anthropology* 37 (2): 257–76.

National Survivors Network. n.d. "Policy/Advocacy." Accessed December 14, 2020. https://nationalsurvivornetwork.org.

Phillips, Alison. 2020. "What I Hope My Sons Learn from the Super Bowl Halftime Show." Exodus Cry, February 4, 2020. https://exoduscry.com.

Provost, Claire, and Lara Whyte. 2018. "Revealed: The US 'Christian Fundamentalists' behind New Netflix Film on Millennial Sex Lives." openDemocracy, May 10, 2018. www.opendemocracy.net.

Roberts, Dorothy E. 2002. *Shattered Bonds: The Color of Child Welfare*. New York: Basic Civitas Books.

Shaw, Ian. 2008. "Ethics and the Practice of Qualitative Research." *Qualitative Social Work* 7 (4): 400–414.

Smith, Melinda. 2018. *Human Trafficking Survivor Leadership in the United States*. Washington, DC: Freedom Network USA.

Soss, Joe, Richard C. Fording, and Sanford Schram. 2011. *Disciplining the Poor: Neoliberal Paternalism and the Persistent Power of Race*. Chicago: University of Chicago Press.

Srikantiah, Jayashri. 2007. "Perfect Victims and Real Survivors: The Iconic Victim in Domestic Human Trafficking Law." *Boston University Law Review* 87:157–211.

Stiles, Siobhan. 2018. "Good versus Evil or 'Saying More': Strategies of Telling in Sex Trafficking Documentary Films." *Journal of Human Trafficking* 4 (1): 35–47.

Vance, Carole S. 2011. "Innocence and Experience: Melodramatic Narratives of Sex Trafficking and Their Consequences for Law and Policy." *History of the Present: A Journal of Critical History* 2 (2): 200–218.

Weitzer, Ronald. 2007. "The Social Construction of Sex Trafficking: Ideology and Institutionalization of a Moral Crusade." *Politics & Society* 35 (3): 447–75.

7

What Gets Lost

At the Intersection of Gender-Based Violence and Racist Scholarship of the Arab Gulf

HASNAA MOKHTAR

An educator in a system of oppression is either a revolutionary or an oppressor.
—Lerone Bennett

I returned from Konya, Turkey, in the summer of 2014, tormented by the mundane tasks of transcribing and analyzing interviews to write my master's thesis. I struggled with my "absolute authority" to make mean-ing of people's intricate stories and life experiences. I shared my inner turmoil about shaping diverse perceptions and encounters into an orga-nized, thematic academic "product" with my advisor and colleagues. *Who am I to do this? What expertise do I have to justify this?* I received the usual responses: "Remain objective, stick with your methodology and theoretical framework, and everything will be fine." But things did not sit right. I wrote the thesis and graduated without ever reconcil-ing the vexing feeling that imperfect human beings could research, diagnose, and craft vulnerable communities' histories in the name of rational, impartial, and scientific knowledge. This chapter begins with that struggle.

While studying the Arab Gulf and researching gender-based violence in Kuwait, I observed how academic research practices sustain struc-tural violence and erase the lived complexities of gendered violence in the region. In this chapter, I highlight several related issues: the gaps in literature on the region, the lack of nuanced representation within the "canon," and how violence is portrayed as an exceptional problem inherent in Gulf communities. To do so, I trace the historical roots of these colonial, orientalist narratives and how they are continually reproduced. Referencing my experiences, I highlight how academic research and practices sustain structural violence and erase the lived complexities of gendered violence, as well as the violent impact this has on addressing researcher entanglements. I discuss Kuwait's Article 153, tracing its colonial history and contemporary violent manifestations as a case study illustrating modern legislative patriarchy or neopatriarchy (Sharabi 1992) in action. I conclude with a call for a relational, decolonial understanding of the region's gender-based violence. My aim is to dialogue about the urgent need for scholarship and policies addressing regional gender-based violence that pay attention to "the connections, entanglements and multiple forms of power configurations that impinge on people's lives" (Al-Ali 2019, 28).

The Struggle of Narrating the "Other"

The struggle I encountered with my master's thesis continued as I contemplated doctoral research. The persistent advice I received was, "Choose one angle and focus there for your dissertation. The rest will come." I knew that my work would focus on gender violence, but how could I choose one of many different, confusing causes globally? As I complete doctoral research, am I more accountable to my discipline's rigidity for for the consequences stemming from the type of knowledge I put into the world? Should I make my doctoral journey easier by prioritizing disciplinary rules or harder by prioritizing my interlocutors?

These questions get more complicated with the geographical region in which I focus and my positionality. I was born in the United States to middle-class Saudi parents and grew up in Saudi Arabia. I am a cisgender, light-skinned, able-bodied survivor of gender-based violence who is visibly Muslim and who wears the *hijab*. While grappling with my trauma and searching for frameworks to understand my experiences with violence, I noticed the substantial lack of unbiased literature concerning gender violence and Arab Gulf countries. English-language literary texts on the region introduced me to rentierism, a masculinist, top-down, gender-blind, and lazy economic theory focused on wealth and oil and their detrimental impact on "democracy," especially in the

Persian Gulf, Middle East, and North Africa (Altunışık 2014; Beblawi 1987, 2016; Gray 2011). Whose democracy? Academic acceptance of these kinds of reductionist theories illustrate how academics are expected to respond to the complexities of this region—to which I am intimately connected and in which I choose to focus my own academic work. I have found that insightful analysis of real-world violence and oppression cannot happen without a critical examination of the violence and oppression upheld through academic practices and within knowledge creation.

The Arab Gulf in the Shadows of Colonial Discourse

Colonial, masculinist, and racist narratives about the Arab Gulf region remain prevalent in modern-day scholarship (AlShehabi 2019). An online search for books on the Arab Gulf yields these topics: rentierism, oil, terrorism, sectarianism, tribalism, monarchies, and authoritarianism. These topics are predominantly addressed through the whitestream, or white mainstream, male gaze. The history of these kinds of connections dates as far back as 1891, when the American Samuel M. Zwemer established the Arabian Mission in "Oman, Bahrain Islands, Kuwait, Basrah Vilayet, Hasa, The Nejd" (Reformed Church 1932, 35). Missionaries created a journal to report regional affairs, naming it *Neglected Arabia* to describe the "remarkable tales of lawlessness, wild adventure and mystery [that] center around these dead cities" (Kellien 1916, 5). They detailed lifeless dunes, depicting the people as "dirty and ragged" (Thoms 1902, 18) with "no moral cleanliness because beastly self-indulgence looks just as good to them as chastity" (Harrison 1916, 15).

The same stereotypical thinking and language—an epistemic violence that I call *Gulf barbarism*—show up in modern-day research on the Arab Gulf. The weight of this epistemic violence makes my research harder: I have to simultaneously maneuver local and global heterosexism while talking back to the whitestream gaze to explain beyond people's ignorance and assumptions. What messages/stories/truths does continuous dehumanization of the Arab Gulf through knowledge production send to the world? What details, differences, and complexities does Gulf barbarism conceal and erase? For what objective or agenda? How does this help anyone understand complex human problems like gender-based violence? I find that this language and knowledge historicize a people according to ideas built from what Toni Morrison (1990) calls the "so-called master narrative," which she describes as a "white male life" that uses "whatever ideological script that is being imposed by the people in authority on everybody else" and that imposes a fictional story on others, built from "a certain point of view." Zak A. Kondo (2020) explains that this one-sided history reinforces the idea that "1. Only white minds can discover things. 2. History began when white man entered the picture. 3. You're supposed to respect some people while [ignoring] others."

The well-crafted rhetoric of Gulf barbarism feeds the colonial project of modernizing the savage while using the region's strategic location and resources. This stereotype is pervasive, because "orientalist ideas about the region, its internal coherence, and its inhabitants unfortunately are still deeply held and often prop up state narratives about who can claim rightful national belonging, what forms of rule are natural, and which histories are legitimate" (Kanna, Le Renard, and Vora 2020, 124). Gulf peoples' voices and struggles, as well as subtle regional differences in gender, religion, class, ethnicity, tribal belonging, education, citizenship status, language, ability, and family origin, are ignored or erased in the common academic story of the region. The impression left is that notable regional history began when the whitestream male gaze acknowledged its existence in writing. Against this backdrop, the complex, multifaceted, global problem of gender-based violence is masked and oversimplified into one of two dichotomous arguments, both of which perpetuate that violence in some way: the reductionist liberal trope about saving victimized Arab Gulf women or the patriarchal Islamic dogma about protecting the piety of Arab Gulf women. Visible violence, such as assault and murder, are discussed in the media and literature in isolation from invisible structural violence, such as racism and heterosexism. It may seem easier this way since there is the potential to identify, arrest, and prosecute a batterer, but ideology that frames women as inferior, *Khaleejis* as savages,[1] and domestic workers as thieves is normalized, weaponized, and built into the social structure without an identifiable face (Galtung 1969).

Ignoring the links between the situational details and broader structural violence, including in academic discourse, maintains an atmosphere ripe for further harming the vulnerable (Menjívar 2015; Piedalue

2015; Al-Ali 2019; Tuck 2009). The scholarly omission of the relational nuances and historical specificities of the dominant, pervasive misrepresentation of *Khaleejis* does a "great damage to all" (Diversi and Moreira 2009, 15). Gender-based violence is a persistent reality for children, women, and men in the Arab Gulf states (Sonbol 2014), and the structural violence represented by this lack exacerbates that violence.

Modern Manifestations of the Colonial History

In March 2018, I attended a meeting with the US assistant secretary of educational and cultural affairs in Kuwait. I was among three Fulbright fellows invited by the US cultural attaché, including an associate professor. Upon the arrival of the assistant secretary, she asked each of us about our work in Kuwait.

> "Kuwaitis are lazy, entitled, ignorant, and way far behind," blurted the white male professor.
>   "Which Kuwaitis exactly are you talking about?" I retorted, warmed by blood rushing to my face.
>   "The US must use its soft powers to push for reforms in this region," he patronizingly contended.

I had met this professor about nine months prior, during the predeparture orientation, where I learned that he was also going to Kuwait. During a session break, I asked why he chose this exchange location, as we both headed to the beverage table for coffee. I vividly remember his blank face, stumbling over his response. He could share neither a strong motive nor a reasonable explanation for his choice, giving the impression of minimal genuine knowledge or interest in the region. I did not think more about his reaction until our conversation with the assistant secretary in Kuwait. Later, previous Fulbright fellows informally shared that the Arab Gulf is a lucrative program destination for Western students and scholars because it pays well. Despite this professor's little genuine interest, inability to speak a single Arabic word, and failure to acknowledge how his privileges (white, male, professor, American, cisgender, and able-bodied) influenced his actions and perspective, in six months he had these racist, degrading, and superficial opinions about

Kuwaitis generally and felt entitled to share them. Attempting to encourage him to stop what felt like an unfounded attack and to self-reflect, I even mentioned the US college-admissions bribery scandal unfolding at that time. But he continued, undeterred from his crusade for the US to "save" a diverse people with a long-standing history of complex moral codes. What granted this professor the prerogative to speak ill of Kuwaitis and not his own people?

Whether with curiosity or sarcasm, I am commonly asked when or if the Arab Gulf region was under colonial rule. I am as regularly shocked to realize that people are surprised by my answer, when discussions of the "empty desert" (Sonbol 2014, 3) are everywhere. Arab Gulf portrayals in Western mainstream media or intellectual settings and texts revolve around terrorism, oil, economy, rentier state, authoritarianism, and so forth. During my graduate work, I noticed the invisibility of the Arab Gulf in campus discussions and syllabi. Only when there was a sudden regional "crisis" was the Gulf mentioned, but through plastered invitations to passively attend an all-white, predominantly male academic discussion. Historically, Arab Gulf countries did not experience militarized or direct colonialism necessitating "the presence of a colonial administration" (Grosfoguel 2011, 15). Instead, the Arab Gulf region experienced indirect rule, subcolonization, or colonization by proxy, "a situation in which 'native' rulers mediated British rule over locals, instead of direct rule by the metropole" (AlShehabi 2019, 30), hence gaining authority and considerable power over the people. Arab Gulf countries were under indirect British colonial rule for over 150 years between 1820 and 1971. Additionally, the Christianizing "Arabian Mission" present in the region as early as 1880 reached Oman, Bahrain, Kuwait, and parts of Saudi Arabia (Al-Sayegh 2014).

This disturbing history of dehumanization through American missionaries, British colonial officers, and Western travelers and researchers writing about the Arab Gulf remains prevalent. Omar AlShehabi highlights similarities between the texts and ideologies of early twentieth-century British colonial officers and English-language texts on the Gulf today (2019, 1). I witnessed similar and recurrent resentment and disgust enacted by whitestream Western foreigners toward locals and mimicked by local elitists toward minority locals, foreign residents, and migrant workers throughout my ten-month doctoral research in Kuwait. The

shield of academia, resting on the Arab Gulf's colonial history and re-
sistant to self-reflection, encourages regurgitating rhetoric used by that
professor in 2018, but it neither explains nor solves the complicated everyday suffering created by gender-based violence.

Legacies of Colonization in Gender Law

Amira Sonbol (2014) argues that Western laws, courts, processes of state
formation, legal codification, and modern capitalism altered the meaning of Gulf societies' Muslim marriages, divorces, and child and family
matters. While women's economic and educational lives have improved
drastically, their lived marital and family realities have worsened (Sonbol 2014, 23). Wael Hallaq (2009) argues that, unlike Westernized
modern laws that sanction and normalize state violence, early Muslim
scholars established their legal norms using reasoned engagement with
Islam's sacred texts, with the goal of promoting tranquility in life and
social interactions. Colonial legacies shift these legal dynamics specifically around gender violence, as Article 153 of Kuwait's Penal Code
demonstrates. For some people, the article concerns family honor, and
for others, it exemplifies how colonial interference in the Arab Gulf has
complicated local contexts for addressing gender violence.

Until 1947, Kuwait was a British protectorate, controlled from British India. Kuwait gained independence in 1961, a year after adopting its
Penal Code, which is still in effect today. The Kuwait legal system combines Islamic law, French civil law, Egyptian law, and British Common
Law, unlike other Arabian countries, which are mainly Islamic states.
Kuwait's Article 153 states that if a man finds his wife or female relative with another man in an adulterous relationship and kills her, her
partner, or both, he will face no more than three years in jail and/or a
fine of around 225 Kuwait dinar. International media and human-rights
agencies describe the article as promoting "honor killing," a problem
often ascribed to Muslims, Islam, and "savage" cultures (Abu-Lughod
2013; Olwan 2013; Razack 2004). In 2014, a group of upper-class Kuwaiti
women started the campaign Abolish Article 153 to contest the article.
The movement founder described this law as "colonial baggage" derived
from the Napoleonic Code's "crime of passion" (Al-Shammaa 2017). In
the 1810 French Civic Code, Article 342 states that a man who, in a fit of

passion, murdered his spouse in the midst of a sexual activity was guilty of no crime. A woman in the same situation was subject to the rigors of the law. Additionally, following Roman legal tradition, a woman found guilty of adultery could be imprisoned for three months to two years, depending on her husband's inclination. A husband convicted of adultery was only subject to a fine of 100 to 2,000 francs (Holmberg 2007).

In 2005 and again in 2014, BBC News reported two separate incidents of Kuwaiti men murdering their daughters. Despite nearly a decade between these reports, BBC News labeled both incidents honor crimes, indicating that "thousands of women are killed by relatives every year in the Middle East and Asia in so-called honor crimes." A quick internet search for similar murders in the US and the West reveals that the label "honor crimes" is never applied to stories in that geographical context. Headlines like "Jealous Father Killed Wife and Children," "Father Admits Beating Daughter to Death Because He Was Jealous," "Jealous Husband Jailed for Life for Killing Wife Who Refused to Sleep with Him," and "Sophie Cavanagh Murder: 'Jealous' Man Jailed for Strangling Wife" (Middleton 2018; Parker 2019; Szathmary 2016) are applied to incidents in the West—but do not mention "honor killings." Lila Abu-Lughod highlights how this label skews relations between men and women where honor is crucial, reinforces the "civilized West versus the barbaric East" trope, and "erases completely the modern state institutions and techniques of governance that are integral to both the incidents of violence and the category by which they are understood" (2013, 113). Dana Olwan adds that this selective labeling is embedded in "'culturalist (and racist) discourses and policy approaches' that hide systematic and institutionalized forms of violence, including the violence of racism" (Olwan 2013, 549, quoting Arat-Koç 2012).

Former US president Donald Trump's 2017 Executive Order 13780, signed under the premise of "Protecting the Nation from Foreign Terrorist Entry into the United States," banned citizens of seven Muslim-majority countries from entering the US and attributed "honor killings" to those who were affected by the ban. The concept of honor killings/crimes originated in the United Nations as early as the 1950s as a "harmful cultural practice" stemming from "customs, ancient laws and practices relating to marriage and the family" (Longman and Bradley 2015, 11). Many scholars have critiqued this labeling, which is often applied to non-Western contexts and stigmatizes cultures and communities instead of specific violent acts. These critiques of customs and rituals are "a familiar repeat of imperial arguments" (Merry 2006, 16) that, as rhetoric disguised as gender equality, intensified the policing of Muslim communities after 9/11 as the "War on Terror" escalated (Abu-Lughod 2013; Razack 2004). This is but one example of how violence against women (interpersonal violence) is linked to colonial legal legacies (coloniality of gender) yet labeled as culturally Islamic and then used to condemn people's worldviews (honor) and justify state violence (terrorists by association).

Many of my 2018–19 Kuwait research participants said that crimes related to Article 153 are not the most pervasive community violence. They questioned Abolish Article 153's agenda, referencing the campaign's founders as representing Kuwaiti society's elites. When asked about this early in the initial campaign, one of Abolish Article 153's founders said to me that they had approached their community members to raise funds and public support. Instead of money or endorsements, the founders were criticized for taking on such a controversial issue. Though difficult to do, the different positionalities and politics of privilege are important to unpack.

Neopatriarchy

In 1740, the politicized Islamic/Wahhabi movement was founded in Saudi Arabia by Muhammad b. 'Abd al-Wahhab, whose stoning of an "adulteress" seemingly solidified his religious authority (Algar 2002). His Saudi and British allies endorsed his persecution and marginalization of women. "This colonial distortion of the Muslim tradition serves as a metaphor for understanding how many interpretations of contemporary Islam circulate today as an authentic Islam whose theological revisions are the result of British and French colonial history in the Muslim world" (Grosfoguel 2017). I learned this history from neither the Saudi government's religious mouthpieces nor the liberal university's self-serving academics. This history needs to be accessible if we are to understand and diminish its persistent violent effects in modern times. "Why is the issue of women's empowerment a red line for the regime? The well-worn explanation lies in the historical symbiosis between Saudi rulers and their Wahhabi clerical supporters: the rulers provide their handpicked ulama with jobs and religious authority, and the ulama provide a cloak for legitimacy for the rulers under the pretense that under Al Saud, religion and state are partners" (Doumato 2011, 206–7). Hisham Sharabi (1992), in line with decolonial feminists such as Chandra Mohanty (2003) and Gayatri Spivak (1995), has argued that white colonizers constructed a powerful inside force in the Arab world by co-opting colonized men into patriarchal roles. "While patriarchies obviously predate colonialism, contemporary patriarchies are products of the intersection between the colonial and indigenous domains of state and political processes. . . . Neopatriarchy concentrates in the petty bourgeois class where it manifests either in the 'progressivism' of Arab socialist regimes or in Islamic fundamentalism" (quoted in Joseph and Slyomovics 2001, 10). Since Saudi Arabia's wealth and position play an instrumental role in shaping the political and social affairs of the region, Wahhabi neopatriarchy has manifested itself through the allegiance between state heads and religious authoritative figures and, by extension, institutions and individuals throughout the Arab Gulf. Women and other marginalized people are the targets of their oppression and violence. Katerina Dalacoura argues that even the persecution of LGBTQI+ people in modern-day Saudi Arabia "derive[s] from European criminal codes, often the Napoleonic codes" (2014, 1296).

Relational and Decolonial Understanding of Gender-Based Violence

No one can effectively discuss or develop Arab Gulf gender violence solutions without unpacking the decades of intentional political and intellectual silencing and marginalization. Regionally nuanced gender violence scholarship must emerge from the Arab Gulf, despite the weight of global capitalist patriarchy, Eurocentric misrepresentation, and state regimes, as an act of reclaiming the right to self-representation and self-determination, "no matter how illiberal" (Mahmood 2005). This focus could encourage those who are marginalized by hegemonic Western research practices to incorporate methodologies embedded in their histories, lived experiences, relational ways of perceiving realities, and value systems (Chilisa 2012). This focus also recognizes the important, legitimate ways that methodological entanglement shows up in the Arab Gulf region, regardless of the gender-based violence researcher's embodiment or the level of nuance they bring to the effort.

I have argued elsewhere that we feminists cannot analyze violence and oppression in the lives of people outside the academy without serious, genuine evaluation of violence and oppression sustained through academic practices and research (Mokhtar and Foley 2020). A feminist (re)evaluation requires us to decolonize our on-campus methods and tools as well as the black-and-white understanding we bring to our gender-based violence research. Our respectful inclusivity must prioritize constructive scholarly critique that aids in understanding gender-based violence broadly. Arab Gulf feminists have argued that "research for the sake of research is a luxury which has no place in the Arab world" (Allaghi and Almana 1984, 34), and I argue that it should not be used to continue to harm the Arab world either.

Addressing What Gets Lost

Gender violence—the processes and actions meant to control, coerce, or otherwise violently exert power over someone because of their gender—was not defined as a human-rights violation until the 1990s (Merry 2006). Since then, feminist scholars, activists, advocates, and practitioners have been on the forefront, drawing attention to and increasing awareness of the problem worldwide. Yet given the complexity and pervasiveness of structural violence, it is no surprise that gender violence has not diminished (Merry 2006). Ever-influential economic inequalities, capitalist greed and white supremacy (including non-Black Arab and *Khaleeji* supremacy, by extension), Islamophobia, xenophobia, and homophobia "have increased rates of gender violence" (Merry 2006, 1–2).

While anyone can be subjected to gender-based violence, Black feminists, led by the Combahee River Collective (1977) and Kimberlé Crenshaw (1989), have provided the foundational "idea that multiple oppressions reinforce each other to create new categories of suffering" (Combahee River Collective 2017, 7). Colonialism, in its physical and structural forms, established both racial and gender hierarchies that necessarily inform the neopatriarchy—a modernized patriarchy where neocolonial forms of patriarchy strike alliances with local patriarchies to dominate specific areas of Arab Gulf society (Sharabi 1992). Hence, US Black feminist thought supports Arab intellectual thought about the neopatriarchy, as gender is central to colonial conceptualization and structural violence. These feminists have also pointed out the violence in knowledge production, or epistemic violence, that denies or diminishes the complexity, agency, and subjectivity of certain populations.

My examination of gender-based violence in Kuwait specifically and the Arab Gulf generally is guided and shaped by this work. And the insightful critiques of US Black feminists illustrate how impossible or ambitious a nuanced, intersectional intervention to address the current literature gap might be. Still, though I am aware that I am barely scratching the surface, I hope that this chapter sparks scholarly and policy conversation about the urgency of nuancing how we address gender-based violence within the Arab Gulf region. Gender violence does not magically appear or develop in a vacuum, so we must historicize this violence to "escape the 'presentism' and myopic views that absolve a wide range of perpetrators, and also historical complicities and silences, as evident in contemporary representations" (Al-Ali 2019, 17). The colonial project, the patriarchal/authoritarian state and politicized Islam, morals and ethics shifted by neoliberal industrialization and the modernization of oil, the still-unsettled Iraqi invasion and Gulf War aftermath, the familial and intergenerational trauma and violence informed cycles, the political maze of privilege, foreign aid and intervention, the injustices against the Bedoon/Bidoon (stateless), domestic workers and laborers, Bedouin marginalization, and homophobia all contribute to the most vile forms of gender-based violence in Kuwait. This has included domestic violence, intimate partner violence, verbal and physical abuse, sexual assault and rape, spiritual and legal abuse, economic violence, and murder. A thorough examination of gender-based violence must consider various local, regional, and global actors' direct and indirect involvement.

There is nothing exceptional about gender-based violence happening in Kuwait or the Arab Gulf region. This violence happens everywhere, including in the most "democratic" countries. There is no such thing as perfect scholarship; however, gender violence researchers and scholars working in this region might consider aiming for exceptionalism in honoring their ethical responsibility and practicing humble self-accountability beyond reflexivity statements and institutional review board approvals. In this context, exceptional and embodied research methodology means attention to researchers' responses to their own investments in the patriarchal and neopatriarchal stories about Arab Gulf realities. Exceptional, embodied research methodology would reject self-righteous, pretentious attitudes among "academic sects that engage in self-affirming research" (Lake 2011, 465) and condemn "the arrogance with which academics construct knowledge about oppression from the comfort of a privileged life" (Diversi and Moreira 2009, 14). Research is about the researcher as much as it is about the researched, because "our understanding of others can only proceed from within our own experience" (Jackson 1989, quoted in Bochner and Ellis, 118). We ought to be "remade" while "engaging in another's worldview" (Mahmood 2005, 36–37). Writing, talking, and presenting about gender-based violence in the Middle East "is very much linked to our respective positionalities, which [shape and influence what] we emphasize in our analysis and findings at any given moment" (Al-Ali 2019, 17). Knowledge created to advance one's rank and income at the expense of flattening multilayered realities by imposing an ill-fitting worldview in the name of rigor is autocratic, predatory scholarship and is violent.

NOTE

1. Gulf Arabic, an Eastern Arabia dialect of Arabic, is commonly referred to as *Khaleeji*, which means "of the Gulf." *Khaleeji* also refers to a sociopolitical identity shared by citizens of the regional, intergovernmental political, and economic union the Cooperation Council for the Arab States of the Gulf, originally known as the Gulf Cooperation Council (GCC). The GCC includes the Arab Gulf states of Bahrain, Kuwait, Oman, Qatar, Saudi Arabia, and the United Arab Emirates.

REFERENCES

Abu-Lughod, Lila. 2013. *Do Muslim Women Need Saving?* Cambridge, MA: Harvard University Press.

Al-Ali, Nadje. 2019. "Feminist Dilemmas: How to Talk about Gender-Based Violence in Relation to the Middle East?" *Feminist Review* 122:16–31. https://doi.org/10.1177/0141778919849525.

Algar, Hamid. 2002. *Wahhabism: A Critical Essay*. Kindle ed. Oneonta, NY: Islamic Publications International.

Allaghi, Farida, and Aisha Almana. 1984. "Survey of Research on Women in the Arab Gulf Region." In *Social Science Research and Women in the Arab World*, 14–40. UNESCO. Paris: Frances Printer.

Al-Sayegh, Fatma. 2014. "Women of the Gulf during the First Half of the Twentieth Century: A Comparative Study of American Missionary Archives and Local Memory." In *Gulf Women*, edited by Amira El-Azhary Sonbol, 241–76. Doha, Qatar: Bloomsbury Qatar Foundation. https://doi.org/10.1111/hisn.12030_6.

AlShehabi, Omar H. 2019. *Contested Modernity: Sectarianism, Nationalism, and Colonialism in Bahrain*. Radical Histories of the Middle East. London: Oneworld Academic.

Al-Shammaa, Khalid. 2017. "Abolish 153 Campaign Seeks to Rid Kuwait for Archaic Law." *Gulf News*, October 20, 2017. http://gulfnews.com.

Altunışık, Meliha Benli. 2014. "Rentier State Theory and the Arab Uprisings: An Appraisal." *Uluslararası İlişkiler* 11 (42): 75–91.

Arat-Koç, Sedef. 2012. "Invisibilized, Individualized, and Culturalized: Paradoxical Invisibility and Hyper-invisibility of Gender in Policy Making and Policy Discourse in Neoliberal CANADA." *Canadian Woman Studies* 29 (3): 6–17.

BBC News. 2005. "Kuwaiti 'Slit Daughter's Throat.'" January 25, 2005. http://news.bbc.co.uk.

———. 2014. "Faleh Ghazi Albasman Detained Indefinitely for Killing Daughter." October 10, 2014. www.bbc.com.

Beblawi, Hazem. 1987. "The Rentier State in the Arab World." In *The Rentier State*, edited by Hazem Beblawi and Giacomo Luciani, 49–62. London: Croom Helm. www.jstor.org/stable/41857943.

———. 2016. "The Concept of 'Rentier States' Revisited." In *The Middle East Economies in Times of Transition*, edited by Ishac Diwan and Ahmed Galal, 199–212. London: Palgrave Macmillan. https://doi.org/10.1007/978-1-137-52977-0.

Bochner, Arthur P., and Carolyn Ellis. 2016. *Evocative Autoethnography: Writing Lives and Telling Stories*. New York: Routledge.

Chilisa, Bagele. 2012. *Indigenous Research Methodologies*. Kindle ed. Thousand Oaks, CA: Sage.

Combahee River Collective. 2017. "The Combahee River Collective Statement." In *How We Get Free: Black Feminism and The Combahee River Collective*, edited by Keeanga-Yamahtta Taylor, 5–14. Chicago: Haymarket Books.

Crenshaw, Kimberlé. 1989. "Demarginalizing the Intersection of Race and Sex: A Black Feminist Critique of Antidiscrimination Doctrine, Feminist Theory and Antiracist Politics." *University of Chicago Legal Forum* 1989:139–67.

Dalacoura, Katerina. 2014. "Homosexuality as Cultural Battleground in the Middle East: Culture and Postcolonial International Theory." *Third World Quarterly* 25 (7): 1290–1306.

Diversi, Marcelo, and Cláudio Moreira. 2009. *Betweener Talk, Decolonizing Knowledge Production, Pedagogy, and Praxis*. Qualitative Inquiry and Social Justice. Walnut Creek, CA: Left Coast.

Doumato, Eleanor Abedlla. 2011. "Women in Civic and Political Life: Reform under Authoritarian Regimes." In *Political Change in the Arab Gulf States: Stuck in Transi-*

tion, edited by Mary Ann Téreault, Gwenn Okruhlik, and Andrzej Kapiszewski, 193–223. Boulder, CO: Lynne Rienner.

Galtung, Johan. 1969. "Violence, Peace, and Peace Research." *Journal of Peace Research* 6 (3): 167–91.

Gray, Mathew. 2011. "A Theory of 'Late Rentierism' in the Arab States of the Gulf." Occasional Paper No. 7, Center for International and Regional Studies, Georgetown University, School of Foreign Service in Qatar.

Grosfoguel, Ramón. 2011. "Decolonizing Post-colonial Studies and Paradigms of Political-Economy: Transmodernity, Decolonial Thinking, and Global Coloniality." *Transmodernity: Journal of Peripheral Cultural Production of the Luso-Hispanic World* 1 (1): 1–37. https://doi.org/10.5070/T411000004.

———. 2017. "Epistemic Islamophobia & Colonial Social Sciences." IRDP Project. https://irdproject.com.

Hallaq, Wael B. 2009. *An Introduction to Islamic Law*. Montreal: McGill-Queens University Press.

Harrison, Paul W. 1916. "The Doctor's Greatest Opportunity." *Neglected Arabia: The Arabian Mission* 99:12–15.

Holmberg, Tom. 2007. "France: Penal Code of 1810." Napoleon Series. www.napoleon-series.org.

Jackson, Michael D. 1989. *Paths toward a Clearing: Radical Empiricism and Ethnographic Inquiry*. Bloomington: Indiana University Press.

Joseph, Suad, and Susan Slyomovics. 2001. Introduction to *Women and Power in the Middle East*, edited by Suad Joseph and Susan Slyomovics, 1–22. Philadelphia: University of Pennsylvania Press.

Kanna, Ahmed, Amélie Le Renard, and Neha Vora. 2020. *Beyond Exception: New Interpretations of the Arabian Peninsula*. Kindle ed. Ithaca, NY: Cornell University Press.

Kellien, Charlottee B. 1916. "Pictures of the Past." *Neglected Arabia: The Arabian Mission* 99:3–5.

Kondo, Zak A. 2020. "A Critique of 'Who Killed Malcom X?'" Public lecture at the Charles H. Wright Museum of African American History, Detroit, MI, June 27, 2020.

Lake, David A. 2011. "Why 'Isms' Are Evil: Theory, Epistemology, and Academic Sects as Impediments to Understanding and Progress." *International Studies Quarterly* 55 (2): 465–80. www.jstor.org/stable/23019696.

Longman, Chia, and Tamsin Bradley. 2015. "Interrogating the Concept of 'Harmful Cultural Practices.'" In *Interrogating Harmful Cultural Practices: Gender, Culture and Coercion*, edited by Chia Longman and Tamsin Bradley, 11–30. Aldershot, UK: Ashgate.

Mahmood, Sabah. 2005. *Politics of Piety*. Princeton, NJ: Princeton University Press.

Menjívar, Cecilia. 2015. "A Framework for Examining Violence." In *Gender through the Prism of Difference*, edited by Maxine Baca Zinn, Pierrette Hondagneu-Sotelo, Michael A. Messner, and Amy M. Denissen, Fifth, 130–44. Oxford: Oxford University Press.

Merry, Sally Engle. 2006. *Human Rights and Gender Violence: Translating International Law into Local Justice*. Chicago: University of Chicago Press.

Middleton, Lucy. 2018. "Jealous Husband Jailed for Life for Killing Wife Who Refused to Sleep with Him." *Metro*, December 10, 2018. https://metro.co.uk.

Mohanty, Chandra Talpade. 2003. *Feminism without Borders: Decolonizing Theory, Practicing Solidarity*. Kindle ed. Durham: Duke University Press.

Mokhtar, Hasnaa, and Ellen E. Foley. 2020. "Advisor–Advisee Feminist Relational Mentoring: A Heartfelt Autoethnographic Conversation." *Feminist Anthropology* 1 (1): 1–18.

Morrison, Toni. 1990. "Toni Morrison on Love and Writing (Part One)." Interview with Bill Moyers, March 11, 1990. https://billmoyers.com.

Olwan, Dana M. 2013. "Gendered Violence, Cultural Otherness, and Honour Crimes in Canadian National Logics." *Canadian Journal of Sociology / Cahiers Canadiens de Sociologie* 38 (4 Park/Santos special issue): 533–56. www.jstor.org/stable/canajsocicahican.38.4.533.

Parker, Charlie. 2019. "Jealous Father Killed Wife and Children." *Times* (London), March 5, 2019. www.thetimes.co.uk.

Piedalue, Amy. 2015. "Understanding Violence in Place: Travelling Knowledge Paradigms and Measuring Domestic Violence in India." *Indian Journal of Gender Studies* 22 (1): 63–91. https://doi.org/10.1177/0971521514556947.

Razack, Sherene H. 2004. "Imperilled Muslim Women, Dangerous Muslim Men and Civilized Europeans: Legal and Social Responses to Forced Marriages." *Feminist Legal Studies* 12:129–74.

Reformed Church. 1932. *One Hundredth Annual Report: Board of Foreign Missions of the Reformed Church in America*. New York: Reformed Church.

Sharabi, Hisham. 1992. *Neopatriarchy: A Theory of Distorted Change in Arab Society*. Oxford: Oxford University Press.

Sonbol, Amira El-Azhary. 2014. "Introduction: Researching the Gulf." In *Gulf Women*, edited by Amira El-Azhary Sonbol, 1–24. Doha, Qatar: Bloomsbury Qatar Foundation. https://doi.org/10.1111/hisn.12030_6.

Spivak, Gayatri Chakravorty. 1995. "Can the Subaltern Speak?" In *The Post-colonial Studies Reader*, edited by Bill Ashcroft, Gareth Griffiths, and Helen Tiffin, 24–28. New York: Routledge.

Szathmary, Zoe. 2016. "Father Admits Beating Daughter to Death Because He Was Jealous." *Daily Mail* (UK), September 16, 2016. www.dailymail.co.uk.

Thoms, Marion Wells. 1902. "Women Patients." *Neglected Arabia: The Arabian Mission* 44:17–20.

Trump, Donald J. 2017. "Executive Order Protecting the Nation from Foreign Terrorist Entry into the United States." https://trumpwhitehouse.archives.gov.

Tuck, Eve. 2009. "Suspending Damage: A Letter to Communities." *Harvard Educational Review* 79 (3): 409–27.

PART III

Witnessing

Entanglements That Humanize Our Methodologies

In part 1, authors named where and how attending to power dynamics through their intimate awareness of their interlocutors' realities enhanced their gender violence research. *Naming* these moments also illuminates the importance of embodied methodology for interrogating what Jennifer R. Wies and Hillary J. Haldane call the enveloping nature of gender violence. In the foreword, Wies and Haldane eloquently explain that "we sometimes no longer see it, the way it clings to us, the way we are shaped by it as we in turn reproduce it in miniature and across scale." To name something requires a shifting awareness and knowing, even if only to distinguish it from the imperceivable, unimaginable, or unspeakable. To name gender violence requires an embodied knowing that shapes our narrativizing as well. The autoethnographic dimension of gender violence research—often devalued in academic methodological training—challenges us to reflect on how our bodies and emotions are associated with the social body. Our passionate engagement reminds us that there is something more than purely cognitive, impersonal pursuits of knowledge. We experience, interact, inhabit, and create narratives about what *is* and what is *not* through the words we utter, through what is named and what is not named. Though the business of academic life may seem to indicate otherwise, the words that form our language tell stories through meaning that evolves across time. The etymology of knowledge—what it is "to know"—clarifies that the foundation of knowledge is that which we witness or perceive with/through our bodies.

According to *The Etymology Dictionary*, the verb "know" is derived from the Old English word *cnawan*. The best translations of *cnawan* explain it as the ability to "perceive a thing to be identical with another," to "be able to distinguish" between things generally, or to "perceive or understand [something] as a fact or truth instead of relying on a belief." Around the year 1200, the word "know" also took on the meaning "to experience, live through." Our language has long indicated that *being* is important to *knowing*.

In part 2, we then turned toward how embodied methodology allows us to recombine the corporeal and conceptual by attending to our ways of *being* in our research. Contributors described being present to the tensions of their interlocutors' experiences before, during, and after research. But that is only part of the presence required. They also described the additional, perhaps more challenging process of being present to oneself in the work, both privately and publicly. These astute contributors point to a deeper knowledge, initiated by distinguishing the various levels of knowing through the naming process. That process—wherein gender violence researchers can identify and verify shared reality—allows researchers to mark the contours of that experience by having lived through it. Thus, the naming process highlights that the ability to "know" anything about gender violence reflects the shifting ability to notice and be *embodied* in the process.

We assert that one of the strengths of embodied methodology is its ability to lean on intersectional specificity to mediate the universality for which academics are told to aim. Living in misogynist societies, we can name the structures that enable gender violence, be they visible or invisible, on every level of our experience (universality). Still, that universal perspective is also violent because it relies on essentialist ideas about who is able to generate concepts and possibilities and to flatten or to ignore others. A tremendous amount of nuanced insight is possible when considering what parts of this violent landscape are visible to whom and to what degree (intersectional specificity). An awareness of how those interlocking, enabling layers of knowledge operates is critical to feminist research generally and gender violence specifically. And while the broad universal perspective may be enough to begin the conversation about concerns, it is never able to fully address a wide-scale, multiprong sociocultural problem like gender-based violence. Attention to the particular realities highlights nuances that, in turn, illuminate the distinct, systemic ways that these violences operate together.

Returning to our etymology, the alchemy between the ability to discern fact from truth in the mind and in the body transforms the possibility of "what it is to know" into "knowledge." *The Etymology Dictionary* indicates that the noun "knowledge" is conceptually linked to the early twelfth-century word *cnawlece*, which translates to "acknowledgment of a superior" as well as "honor, worship." Breaking up the word, *cnaw-* refers to the "act of knowing." The second part of *cnawlece (-lece)* is obscure, perhaps Scandinavian, and is linguistically cognate (or sharing its origin) with *-lock*, indicating an "action, process," as in wedlock. In this sense, knowledge can be understood as a process of coming to know by honoring what we perceive through our being.

From the late fourteenth century, "knowledge" has also been used to indicate the "awareness of or capacity for knowing, understanding; [a] familiarity," and "news, notice, information; learning; an organized body of facts or teachings." Awareness of the processes that organize perceptions into a multifaceted, complex story of collective experience is key to the transformation of knowing into knowledge. To engage knowledge, we must search out and witness others' processes of coming to know as well as our own.

Anthropology and sociology frequently encourage us to hold sacrosanct the disciplinary charge to serve as a witness to trends and meaning-making that radiate outward from individuals to systems. These trends structure ongoing events such as colonialism (Tuck and Yang 2012) and back inward in an infrequently disrupted loop. As suggested previously, that loop is necessarily altered in some fashion by the humans who experience it as research participants (our interlocutors). That loop is also altered by those who experience it as "subjected participant/observer" (Petillo and Hlavka, chapter 1 in this volume). Every contributor in this volume, including the editors, recognized themselves in multiple aspects of their interlocutors' experiences because of our corporeal cultural and social realities. These realities, carried with our skin, religious practices, physical and neurological makeups, kin/relationships, languages, and geographies, brought us closer to relative truths about gender violence instead of farther away. In that sense, "academic" and "researcher" are included in our realities. As we experience, perceive, and interpret through our positionalities, we must remember that these filters do not absolve us from the realities of being the humans we are when we leave academic halls. Gender violence research concerns the politics of what is felt (Million 2009). As with our interlocutors, we are subject to violation "in the field," be it situated across an ocean, in a courtroom, or from a familiar face. Gender violence research also equally concerns what we "search for" in what others feel, know, and carry as knowledge.

The story of the search for knowledge is also tied up in its etymology. The noun "research" refers to the act of "searching closely," a meaning traced to the 1570s. The English noun comes from the French *recerche*, which originates from the Old French verb *recercher*—meaning to "seek out, search closely." The foundation combines the prefix *re-* ("back to the original place; again, anew, once more" with an accompanying sense of "undoing") and the root verb *cercher* ("to seek for" from the Latin *circare*, which translates as "go about, wander, traverse, to wander hither and thither"). The evolution of the word/story of research rested on the cyclical activity of considering and reconsidering the meaning of "scientific inquiry" in the 1630s. This book's contributors illustrate the story of *knowledge*, as revealed in its etymology, through a demonstration of embodied methodology in gender violence research.

When interlocutors share their experiences with researchers, there is an expectation about what we will do with that knowing (Davis 2013). We assert that the expectation is to turn what we then know into useful, actionable knowledge. Some of that action involves active witnessing—not just as a participant-observer but also as one who is unsettled (Fukushima 2016). As discussed in this book's introduction and conclusion, Annie Fukushima reframes witnessing as active, instead of passive, a commitment to refuse "being settled with what one is seeing. Unlike spectators, witnesses are called to action." Annie Fukushima includes "raising questions about normative aspects of events as well as examining the politics of representation surrounding victimhood/criminality, citizenship, and legality as they are infused with the discourse of nationhood, race, and gender" (2006, 148). Contributors in this part of the book use embodied methodology to answer that call to witness actively. As researchers unsettled by what we see, we are also unsettled in our self-witnessing (or experience).

Unsettled witnessing is the ability to respond and cocreate from embodied engagement.

As this part's contributors demonstrate, such interlocutor and researcher witnessing facilitates intersectional knowledge of situation and systems. This witnessing also makes visible the impacts on personhood beyond the system-structuring. Witnessing reveals the ongoing narratives that construct victim/survivors as one-dimensional beings to be pitied, gender violence researchers as one-dimensional "touchy-feely" academics, and both as mutually exclusive experiences. We suspect that once you have engaged an entangled, embodied methodology in gender violence research by doing the following, you will experience shifts in your research, knowledge, and awareness similar to those detailed by the contributors in this final part:

- Naming where interlocutors' realities, researcher embodiment, and the research power inequities meet
- Marking where multilayered being informs what is possible and remaining open to that as a source of important insight
- Moving from that knowledge to burrow deeper into the research as an unsettled witness across nuances and entanglements

Jamie L. Small's interrogation of her experience studying elite populations in the context of sexual violence research, "'Just a Darling Little Girl': Attorneys, Power, and Notes from the Field in Research on Sexual Violence," begins this part of the book. In chapter 8, Small describes her experience of gendered processes and performances in interviews with attorneys working on sexual assault cases, reflecting on how these gendered interactions and ideologies embedded in the process influence knowledge production. Engaged in "studying up," Small reveals the power dynamics that unfold when the researched have more power than the researcher. Together, these processes risk privileging hegemonic discourses, but they also draw our attention to the ideological inadequacies of university institutional review boards that routinely deny how power can shift between researcher and participants.

In chapter 9, "Trauma-Informed Research Methods: Understanding and Healing Embodied Violence," Noelle Brigden recognizes how her own trauma and recovery directly and indirectly informed her research methods and relationship building with interlocutors. In the process of fieldwork interrupted by what has been an extended period of global trauma in response to the COVID-19 pandemic, Brigden notes how the outward read of her embodied trauma was weaponized against her interlocutors. In the process of witnessing, she notes how structural violences give passage to emotional violence, social inequities, lack of care, and lateral hostilities that leave physical markers on her interlocutors' gendered bodies and lives. Brigden illustrates how trauma provides a conceptual tool for locating struggle and social fragmentation in the body and builds an embodied methodology for healing.

In chapter 10, "Intersectionality in the Courts: Collaborative Feminist Ethnography of Sexual Assault Adjudication," the last of this section, Amber Joy Powell, Sameena Mulla, and Heather R. Hlavka write about their fieldwork experiences as a racially and ethnically diverse ethnographic team and how social positionality accounts for visible and invisible ethnographic tools. The authors engage with intersectionality and embodiment as a critical social theory of power relations that structures courtroom interactions. They describe the uneven purchase of power and domination in criminal prosecution, among both participants and the researchers, and thereby valorize feminist collective, team-based, and embodied research methodologies.

Together these chapters invoke somatic/body consciousness. The authors describe the physical and emotional practices and changes enacted to fit into their research fields and to transform their field sites, as well as the numerous ways in which their bodies were read, perceived, and used—sometimes alongside their interlocutors. The body, in the chapters in this part, is witness to itself; it is somatic awareness (Shusterman 2005). Reflecting on bodies and witnessing our own and other bodies as they come to be understood outside of ourselves not only creates a somatic consciousness and embodied knowledge but also produces better research on gender violence.

REFERENCES

Davis, Dána-Ain. 2013. "Border Crossings: Intimacy and Feminist Activist Ethnography in the Age of Neoliberalism." In *Feminist Activist Ethnography: Counterpoints to Neoliberalism in North America*, edited by Christa Craven and Dána-Ain Davis, 23–38. Lanham, MD: Lexington Books.

Fukushima, Annie Isabel. 2016. "An American Haunting: Unsettling Witnessing in Transnational Migration, the Ghost Case, and Human Trafficking." *Feminist Formations* 28 (1): 146–65.

Million, Dian. 2009. "Felt Theory: An Indigenous Feminist Approach to Affect and History." *Wicazo Sa Review* 24 (2): 53–76.

Shusterman, Richard. 2005. "The Silent, Limping Body of Philosophy." In *The Cambridge Companion to Merleau-Ponty*, edited by Taylor Carman and Mark B. N. Hansen, 151–80. Cambridge: Cambridge University Press.

Tuck, Eve, and K. Wayne Yang. 2012. "Decolonization Is Not a Metaphor." *Decolonization: Indigeneity, Education & Society* 1 (1): 1–40.

8

"Just a Darling Little Girl"

Attorneys, Power, and Notes from the Field in Research on Sexual Violence

JAMIE L. SMALL

It was cooler weather than I expected for Manhattan in July. The temperature was falling, and rain was expected for that afternoon, when I would be somewhere in Queens for my second appointment. Walking up Eighth Avenue in the morning, I was mentally reviewing my interview guide and my physical appearance. Both were equally important. I checked and rechecked my phone for the address and finally found my destination. The building was sleek and modern and stunning. I walked through the doors, quickened my step, and strode toward the security turnstiles. I scanned the lobby to assess if there were any unspoken procedures of which I should make myself aware. I did not want to make a fool of myself—both for the sake of my ego and for the sake of not jeopardizing my entry into this exclusive law firm. A security guard confirmed my appointment with a secretary upstairs and gave me a name badge. I rode the elevator up high and entered the most serene and beautiful office space. A paralegal greeted and then guided me to a conference room. She left me alone, and I had a moment to relax. As I gazed out the window and soaked in the city from that majestic bird's-eye view, someone else wheeled in a beverage service. Cookies, tea, coffee, soda, crackers, water—and with proper dishes, no less. It struck me as rather extravagant for a conversation of two.

Conducting interviews with elite actors requires a unique navigation of power dynamics that unfold in the data-collection process. In this chapter, I ask, How and where does power emerge in research involving elite actors? Moreover, when studying male-dominated professions, like law, how do those power dynamics become gendered? My discussion spans two different research projects, one that focused on county-level prosecutions of male-male rape and another that focused on a high-profile case of police brutality and sexual assault. In total, I conducted eighty-seven qualitative interviews with sex-crime prosecutors, defense attorneys, and several other related legal actors. Interviews were conducted in Michigan, Georgia, Idaho, and New York. Just over 80 percent of respondents were men, which is not surprising, given the gender composition of criminal law practice in the United States. I also draw briefly on my experiences in the historical archives. In the following discussion, I use pseudonyms and obscure any potentially identifying details. This autoethnographic account of the data-collection process is not intended to be prescriptive or exhaustive. Rather, I present a kaleidoscope of moments from the field to sketch out broader observations about gender, power, and the creation of knowledge. The following discussion is organized chronologically based on the data-collection process: preparations, conducting interviews, challenges in the field, and then unexpected consequences. I close with an observation of the reverberating effects that emerge when witnessing sexual trauma.

Epistemologies of Violence

My discussion is informed primarily by two different literatures: feminist methodology and sociology of elites. Feminist scholars from a range of disciplines critique the logics of scientific objectivity (Haraway 1988; Harding 1991). They argue that achieving objectivity is not only impossible but also a dangerous illusion because it positions the scientist as an outsider to the social world. By elevating the scientist to a position of all-knowing and benevolent, the model of scientific objectivity tends toward a Western male gaze (Collins 1986). But eliding politics does not make them disappear. Even the very questions that we ask are shaped by the historical and material conditions in which they emerge (Fausto-Sterling 2000). To be sure, the tentative resolution to these points is not to disregard empirical evidence altogether but rather to recognize that it is always partial and situated.

Yet, while feminist methodologists are deeply concerned with issues of power at all stages of the research process, they tend to focus on the challenges that come with studying marginalized groups (Reissman 1987; Stacey 1988). There is little recognition of circumstances in which researchers hold relatively less power than the populations they are studying. Here, the recent turn in sociology to studying elite populations is instructive (Hartmann 2006; Khan 2012). Similar to feminist methodologists, qualitative sociologists (the two groups are not mutually exclusive, to be sure) have historically focused on marginalized groups. Building on the foundation laid by the Chicago School of sociologists in the mid-twentieth century, the point of this intellectual work was to decenter powerful groups and examine the lives and patterns of ordinary people. But ultimately, the cultural milieu and decisions of powerful people have a disproportionate impact on the social world. While we want to avoid aggrandizing them, we also cannot risk ignoring them.

Many of the respondents in my sample would probably not consider themselves to be "elite." It is more likely that they would categorize themselves as ordinary people. Yet their positions in the legal field meant that their decisions carried outsized influence—not just in the various lives of sexual victims or perpetrators but also with regard to constructing what we know about sexual violence in the first place.

Preparation: Identity Work and "Me-Search"

When I started interviewing attorneys, midway through my doctoral program, I was primarily interested in gender and sexuality. Law was an entry point for some broader questions about which I was curious but was not necessarily my main focus. Moreover, I had not gone to law school and had no plans to do so. This meant that I was quite nervous when I set out to collect data. I was uncertain about how many respondents I would be able to recruit, and I was apprehensive about how they might respond to me, especially since I looked quite young at the time.

To prepare for the interviews, I worked on a mitigation strategy to regender myself. I bought some new clothes that looked "lady professional." I practiced speaking with more authority. I tried to walk with longer strides and a sense of purpose. I followed the advice of one mentor, who recommended wearing nice jewelry but avoiding bracelets that would distract and clank on tabletops. In essence, I was arranging my body in a way that was similar to what one of my future respondents recommended her victims do in preparation for their courtroom testimony. She said, "You [sexual assault victims] should wear what you would wear to church. . . . We don't want the cleavage showing. You want to be covered up. Dresses need to be a little longer if you're going to wear skirts. Try to dress appropriately for the season. So don't come in a tank top and short shorts. You're coming to court, so slacks or jeans are fine. But let's not have them all ripped up." As a researcher, I did not have the luxury of settling for jeans, but the logic was the same: the courthouse necessitates a visual politics of respectability. Mine was ultimately a performance of gender that magnified certain elements of femininity while simultaneously distancing me from the iconic category of vulnerable woman.

The process of regendering myself for the field included affective components in addition to the physical transformations. I felt that I needed to distance myself from revealing any emotionality or vulnerability. So much writing on sexual violence—indeed, some of our most important interventions (Gay 2018; Miller 2019)—is based on experiential knowledge. However, with some notable exceptions (e.g., Brison 2003), there is a sharp bifurcation between experiential and scholarly knowledge about sexual violence. The former is widely considered anecdotal and singular, whereas the latter is considered more objective and reliable. While multiple data points are necessary to identify social patterns across different times, places, and groups, adhering to a scientific model of data collection also has the collateral consequence of upholding an illusion that the researcher is not invested in the object of study. This is a difficult illusion to maintain when studying an issue like sexual violence, where the specter of gendered corporeal harm is omnipresent. Yet in my case, the question of whether I was doing "me-search"—a disparaging characterization of research that is perceived to be motivated primarily by the researcher's biography—never came up. This may be due to the fact that in both projects, I was studying men who were sexually victimized; and I present as a normatively feminine woman, so I was clearly not studying my own group. Or perhaps my performance of professionalism was just so convincing that my respondents did not see me as potentially sexually vulnerable. So the interview conversations proceeded as though we all existed above the criminal fray: those who occupied this professional sphere were neither victims nor perpetrators.

As I moved through the research process, however, I started to question these sharp distinctions of how individuals were oriented toward the problem of sexual violence. In my dissertation, I discussed briefly on how I did not identify as a survivor of sexual assault. At the time, it felt like an important disclosure to make. Although I had adhered to rigorous social science methods of data collection and analysis, I was also deeply embedded in literature on feminist methodology, which, in broad strokes, advances the position that scholars *should* disclose their relationship to their research topics. When I wrote that paragraph, years into research on sexual violence, I still conceptualized survivorship as a dichotomous category: either you had been raped, or you had not been raped. It seemed like a distinct, obvious, and knowable thing.

But several semesters into my faculty position, I began to question my swift conclusion. I had the opportunity to teach a lower-level course on sexual violence, and I incorporated smaller units in many of my other courses as well. As I guided my students through discussions about the thorniness of sexual consent, I started to rethink some of my own sexual experiences. There had been times when I was entirely too intoxicated to provide any sort of consent; there had been times when a partner engaged in excessive badgering to wear me down; and there had been a couple of times involving so much aggression that I was scared. None of those experiences in the moment had felt like what I thought of as sexual assault, but in each event, there was undoubtedly a lack of respect for my sexual autonomy, at minimum. Given the enduring patriarchal norms of US society, it should probably not be surprising that the disconnect between what we see as ordinary heterosexual encounters and sexual assault—even for a feminist researcher—is so slippery.

Data Collection: Building Rapport and Breaking the Fourth Wall

The vast majority of the minutes that I spent with respondents were structured by the ordinary norms of professional collegiality. Although I was an outsider and substantially younger than most of them, they treated me as a respected colleague. They were responsive, kind, and generous with their time. Many of them reported afterward that they enjoyed the conversations because it gave them an opportunity to reflect on their work and careers. Given my apprehension at the outset of both rounds of data collection, this was a great relief. It probably did not hurt that I was a white woman affiliated with a prestigious university.

On occasion, however, the professional decorum was punctuated by a momentary lapse into a different mode of interaction. The interviews were intentionally conversational; I had a structured list of questions that I needed to cover, but there was also plenty of space for meandering stories along the way. Collectively, these meandering stories generated important insights about sexual assault prosecutions in the United States. There was one respondent who, at the end of his career, had considerable experience in a variety of different legal roles, including prosecution and defense at both trial and appellate levels. In the course of our conversation, I asked him how he maintained empathy for criminal defendants who had been accused of horrifically violent acts. He replied that he tried to picture them as children: "I can see how they looked when they were six. I can see how *you* looked when you were six: just a darling little girl. And if you can see that person—that person's still inside there. I have a view that there is no time and that it's sort of a figment of our imagination, and that's the way we organize our experiences in the world. So that person at six years old is still there." Given Western ideologies of childhood innocence, this strategy of humanization is ostensibly an effective strategy: the child buried deep within the criminal still deserves his lawyer's concern, hard work, and recognition. However, this brief anecdote also reoriented our professional exchange. An imaginary version of my six-year-old self had entered the space. I had not expected to meet that ghost during the interview, and it made me feel self-conscious. Although not mean-spirited, the comment felt paternalistic. Being characterized as a "darling little girl" reminded me of my relative subordinate status. In the span of seconds, I had shifted from a scientific researcher to a little girl.

This moment in which we broke through the proverbial "fourth wall" reveals the tenuous nature of the interview interaction. It is a scripted social encounter crafted by the interviewer, but when the respondents are also skilled interviewers, the ebb and flow of the conversation is more horizontal than it would be across a hierarchical power dynamic. As we shall see in the next section, these breaks in professional civility are not always benign.

Difficult Encounters: Vulnerability and Getting Kicked Out of Offices

During graduate school, I received considerable training on how to recognize and account for the power dynamics involved in sociological research. In a qualitative methodology course, we focused on equitable recruitment strategies for vulnerable communities and the relationship of the researcher's identity and biography to the subjects of analysis. In a feminist methodology course, we focused on what it meant for privileged individuals from well-resourced universities to study marginalized populations, especially across transnational borders. Gayatri Spivak (1988) wondered if the subaltern could ever speak, especially within the disciplining parameters of Western ideologies, of which the social science fields belong. In essence, my professors were asking me to think deeply about "studying down." Yet none of this intellectual work prepared me for my eightieth interview and "studying up."

I did not have this interview scheduled in advance. I was eager to speak with Michael, but he had not replied to my two recruitment emails. So I called his office to follow up when I had some open time in the research week. The receptionist put me through to his direct line, which was surprising, and I pitched my project. I told him what the interview would entail and explained why his perspective was important. He invited me to his office the following afternoon. Considering that it was basically a cold call, the whole thing was oddly easy.

The attorneys whom I interviewed worked in a wide range of office spaces, from glitzy urban skyscrapers to ramshackle cubbies tucked away in small towns. Aside from the expensive address, though, Michael's office was relatively modest: a midsized waiting room that opened onto a hallway of a handful of enclosed offices. It was unremarkable. What was notable, however, were the photographs, hundreds of them. They lined the walls in perfectly measured grids, from the waiting room and then snaking into the hallway and the adjoining offices. They were black-and-white photographs of Michael posing with various famous people—politicians, celebrities, and musicians. His was clearly a well-connected life. Individually, they were nice: elegant portraits and snapshots framed gallery-style. Collectively, they were overwhelming. They swallowed the space whole and felt like physical evidence of an outsized ego.

As the receptionist led me into Michael's office, I saw him perched behind an expansive desk, wearing a perfectly styled suit and accessories to match. We shook hands, and I sat down on one of the chairs facing his desk. Although we had spoken on the phone just the day before, I explained the research project again. Then I explained the informed-consent procedures, and I handed him the form that required his signature. This is where things took a turn for the worse. Michael asked why I needed his signature and what it would be used for. His tone shifted rapidly from one of warmth to one of hostility. Anticipating that he might be taking me for a muckraking journalist, I tried to pivot and clarify, ever so briefly, that I was a sociologist. I was bound by the ethical guidelines of scientific research and therefore simply needed to confirm that he was an informed and willing participant in the study. That was all and everything that the signature was about—crucial for me, and for the profession, but, in reality, probably not terribly important for him, considering his stature and power. Yet it was a sticking point. He became deeply suspicious of me.

The more I tried to explain, the more suspicious he became, and then he became angry. He was skilled at projecting aggressive masculine energy, no doubt developed over many years of working in a cutthroat legal environment. He tossed the consent form across the desk, and he warned that he would not introduce me to other people involved in the case, never mind that I had not asked for such a favor. I felt intimidated. He had broken the norms of professional civility so suddenly and unexpectedly. I tried to maintain my composure and uphold my ethical obligations. It was clear by then that the research interview was not going to happen, and this was his extremely assertive way of saying, "I do not consent." He asked me to leave, and I did.

At that point in my career, I had conducted dozens of research interviews. Michael's response was singular, and it left me rattled. Some respondents asked follow-up questions after my explanation of informed consent, and a couple of respondents requested that small portions of our conversation be redacted. But none of them had responded with anger. Moreover, they were all sophisticated enough to understand roughly what they had agreed to with the interview appointment (which certainly does not mean that they could not withdraw their consent partway through, but the nature of the interview itself should not have been surprising). One might offer different accounts for Michael's negative reaction: Perhaps he was having a bad day. Perhaps his was a generally difficult personality. Perhaps he had had bad experiences with journalists in the past and so was justifiably skeptical of my intentions. Perhaps there were regional differences in our expectations of professional civility. Perhaps he was a misogynist who was accustomed to treating women poorly.

Michael's extraordinary way of declining to participate illuminates the inverted power dynamics of research with elite actors. Most discussions about ethics in research focus on how to ensure the safety and autonomy of vulnerable populations—rightly so, given the substantial harm caused by ethical violations in the past. This paradigm assumes that the researcher is in a position of power relative to their study participants. Yet these dynamics simply did not exist in my data-collection process. If anything, I held relatively less power than most of my respondents. I was younger—by several decades, in many cases—and a woman without a law degree. To be sure, my institutional affiliations connoted social status; and my role as a professor in the second set of interviews engendered respect from respondents. Nonetheless, the more formidable challenge was not minimizing my interactional power during the interview but rather *maximizing* it. I needed to demonstrate, within seconds of meeting each participant, that I was their equal; had I been too deferential, it is almost certain that they would have been dismissive.

Institutional review boards (IRBs) are ill equipped to address this issue. For the dissertation interviews, the IRB panel gave my project heightened scrutiny. They were concerned that my questions might cause harm because I was asking about sexual violence. It took months of revisions to finally secure approval. One of the conditions was that I had to distribute fliers to respondents that provided them with a list of antiviolence resource agencies, should they require therapeutic support after the interview. For university administrators concerned with risk management, this approach made sense. On the ground, however, it turned out to be the most uniformly awkward part of all the interviews because my respondents already knew about their community's resources. When I handed the flier to one prosecutor, she reproached me: "You're missing a very important one [social service agency]. . . . You should note that." She made her local expertise clear, rightly so, because as an outsider, I simply did not know nearly as much. Moreover, the professional culture of criminal prosecution and defense work is fast paced and masculine; there is generally little space or incentive for individuals to display emotions that would reveal vulnerability. So the likelihood that one of my respondents would have sought the therapeutic services recommended on my flier—the very places to which they sent their own victims and clients—seemed very low, indeed.

Consequences: Vicarious Trauma and the Complexity of Witnessing

Long after data collection for my dissertation had ended, I was on a conference panel where we were discussing gender and human rights. After the panelists each offered some introductory remarks, we opened it up to audience questions. Several of my students were in the audience because the conference was at my home institution. One of them asked how we dealt with the emotional challenges of researching sexual violence. It was a tough question. My immediate answer was that it settles in your bones; the trauma stories take root in your being and create an altered self. Although I did not appreciate it at the time, the year that I spent conducting dissertation interviews, when my daughter was two years old, was deeply unsettling. It was also one of the most exciting and stimulating years of my life.

As a graduate student, I could only afford part-time child care for my daughter, three days per week. Her father's job came with more conventional hours, where he was bound to the office, so I shouldered most of the burden of covering the rather large gap between our child-care and working hours. Between teaching, data collection, and caring for a toddler, my schedule was packed. Geographically, I was also spread thin: I conducted all interviews, save for one, in person, which meant that I was spending many, many hours in rental cars crisscrossing Michigan, Georgia, and Idaho. I had virtually no time to decompress or process the trauma stories in which I was swimming. When I finally finished all the interviews, right after my daughter celebrated her third birthday, my body stopped. Once the momentum of the interview timetable was gone, I could do no more. It was as if I had hit a brick wall. This breakdown coincided with the collapse of my marriage, which was due, among other things, to the strains of scarcity—we were woefully short on time, money, and compassion. During those months, my emotions were so frazzled that all work tasks had become completely overwhelming, and the prospect of writing a dissertation seemed laughable. I barely wrote anything in the year following the interviews.

The strange thing about my interview sets, though, was that their trauma narratives were refracted by legal logics. Not only were the stories of pain not my own lived experience, but they were also mediated by the structures and priorities of criminal prosecution. Moreover, I often uncovered the trauma narratives in fragmented form—a brief anecdote during an interview or a set of case facts, necessarily limited, presented in a police report. It seems probable that some of the legally polished narratives of harm might not even have felt familiar to the victims themselves.

The reverberating effects of this trauma imagery extended far beyond the people interacting directly with it—both in the legal case and in the research process. I had assumed, naïvely perhaps, that the difficulties of my scholarship could be contained, but they spilled out in surprising ways. The summer when my daughter was nine years old, she attended a day camp while I worked. She came home agitated one evening: another child had swiped a special bottle of hand sanitizer that dangled from her backpack. I acknowledged that this was an unkind action and that if the bottle could not be retrieved, then we would buy a replacement. It seemed like a relatively trivial issue, particularly for my normally easy-going kid, but she remained upset. As we read bedtime stories, I inquired further about why she had such strong feelings about the hand sanitizer. She revealed that the girl who took it was mean, kind of a bully, and so we talked about how there were only two days left in the camp, after which she would never see the girl again. She nodded her head, but I could tell that she was still spinning on something. I asked her more about the girl. Who was she? What was she like? Was she mean to all the kids?

My daughter reported that this bully-girl was mean to all the kids. I noted that sometimes when kids are mean, it is a consequence of other people, maybe their parents or family members, not treating them kindly. Maybe this bully-girl was experiencing her own difficulties, which caused her to act out in cruel ways. My daughter seized on this interpretation; yes, the bully-girl had told her something, a secret. I asked what the girl had told her, and my daughter clammed up, an odd reaction for a chatterbox. I kept pressing her, gently, because it seemed like she wanted to get this information off her chest. She said that something had happened to the bully-girl, like what I study. At this point, I paused. I did not know how much my daughter knew about my writing. I always left books and papers scattered around the house, and she often came to work with me when her school was closed. But I had never talked directly to her about sexual violence, other than occasional conversations about children's bodily autonomy and the importance of consent for physical touching. I asked her to be more specific. She hedged and stammered, and finally she said that the word starts with an *r*. Okay. I asked her to type the whole word into my phone; I wanted her to say whatever it was that she had to say in her own words. She typed, "r-a-p." Then, she said, "Like that, but with an *e*." Spelling was not my daughter's best subject, but she was saying clearly that this bully-girl had disclosed to her that she had been raped.

Once again, I was startled. I was deeply concerned for this child and collected as much information as possible to share with the camp director and our child advocacy center. But I was also curious that my daughter had somehow picked up knowledge about sexual violence, over all these years of tertiary immersion. The trauma and violence and trouble in finding an adequate language of description had not escaped her view. I do not believe that children should be shielded from the unjust aspects of social life, but it was still hard to have such a stark reminder of how much these things ooze and spread. My bearing witness and messy attempts to identify patterns of violence had infused her childhood. For better and for worse.

Conclusions: Situated Bodies and the Pervasiveness of Violence

My flight to New Jersey was inexplicably delayed by four hours. It was early August and a midday flight, so I had not expected to have so many extra minutes to dawdle in the Columbus airport. The delay meant that I would miss spending a night at the beach with a good friend and her family. It was to have been some hours of leisure before heading to Manhattan for a week of research on sexual violence. Instead, I found a cheap hotel in Newark and ate dinner by myself at the bar. It was an early night. When I first started stirring at dawn the next morning, I was a bit disoriented because the previous day had been such a shuffle. It took me a minute to remember where I was and why. I glanced at my phone and was surprised to see two messages from old friends asking if I was okay. Something must have happened. I looked at the news and quickly figured out that there had been a mass shooting one mile north of my house in Dayton.

While I was sleeping in Newark, twenty-four-year-old Connor Betts shot and killed nine people, just hours after another mass shooting in El Paso, Texas. Most of the victims had been socializing outdoors in the popular Oregon District, and because it was a hot summer night, panic and chaos spread quickly throughout the neighborhood. Nearby police officers shot Betts within a minute of his attack, bringing the total number of dead to ten people. In the days following, several of Betts's former classmates reported that he had been suspended during high school for allegedly writing on a bathroom wall a "hit list" of boys he wanted to kill and girls he wanted to rape. Other evidence emerged that he was fixated on violent imagery that depicted women's bodies.

All of this occurred on the eve of a demanding week of data collection. It was difficult to process this seemingly sudden act of violence near my home from such a distance. I let myself wander aimlessly around lower Manhattan on Sunday afternoon, but by bedtime, I had to bracket those emotions so that I could focus on my work. Conducting qualitative interviews requires intensive focus, and the attorneys had tight schedules. There was no time for more dawdling or therapeutics. But the shooting still threaded through my experience of that week of data collection—how could it not?—and remained a stark reminder of the violent power that men still wield.

REFERENCES

Brison, Susan J. 2003. *Aftermath: Violence and the Remaking of a Self*. Princeton, NJ: Princeton University Press.

Collins, Patricia Hill. 1986. "Learning from the Outsider Within: The Sociological Significance of Black Feminist Thought." *Social Problems* 33 (6): 14–32.

Fausto-Sterling, Ann. 2000. *Sexing the Body: Gender Politics and the Construction of Sexuality*. New York: Basic Books.

Gay, Roxane, ed. 2018. *Not That Bad: Dispatches from Rape Culture*. New York: Harper Perennial.

Haraway, Donna. 1988. "Situated Knowledges: The Science Question in Feminism and the Privilege of Partial Perspective." *Feminist Studies* 14 (3): 575–99.

Harding, Sandra. 1991. *Whose Science? Whose Knowledge? Thinking from Women's Lives*. Ithaca, NY: Cornell University Press.

Hartmann, Michael. 2006. *The Sociology of Elites*. New York: Routledge.

Khan, Shamus Rahman. 2012. "The Sociology of Elites." *Annual Review of Sociology* 38:361–77.

Miller, Chanel. 2019. *Know My Name: A Memoir*. New York: Viking.

Reissman, Catherine Kohler. 1987. "When Gender Is Not Enough: Women Interviewing Women." *Gender & Society* 1 (2): 172–207.

Spivak, Gayatri Chakravorty. 1988. "Can the Subaltern Speak?" In *Marxism and the Interpretation of Culture*, edited by Cary Nelson and Lawrence Grossberg, 271–313. Basingstoke, UK: Macmillan.

Stacey, Judith. 1988. "Can There Be a Feminist Ethnography?" *Women's Studies International Forum* 11 (1): 21–27.

9

Trauma-Informed Research Methods

Understanding and Healing Embodied Violence

NOELLE BRIGDEN

Decades ago, before I ever imagined I would become a researcher, I shattered a vertebra. After nearly a year of physical therapy, I walked away from the hospital and into a new life, thanks to a medical discharge from the US military and a veterans' disability program that encouraged me to study. This lucky break caused me to reevaluate my own militarization, internalization of patriarchy, and violent masculinity: a fortuitous rupture in all that I had previously taken for granted. Grappling with the limits of my body changed me profoundly. However, over a decade later, my fieldwork on violence along the migration route from El Salvador across Mexico exacerbated the chronic pain from this injury. Compounded by emotional trauma and years of searching for physical relief, I began to lift weights and to embrace strength and growth over my body insecurities and deep shame. Eventually, I taught powerlifting and calisthenics at my field sites in El Salvador, founding a community gym that has reshaped my research trajectory (Brigden 2021). Like Susan Wendell (1996), who examines the nature of disability starting with her own experience, confrontation with my physical limitations led to a series of feminist reflections about violence and methodology. In the process of discovering my own fitness rituals to cope with multiple personal traumas, I also began to encourage other people to move with me. One of the first women I encouraged was my friend Gloria. For a time, we shared walks.

Frankly, it took me too long to realize how Gloria's experience and our friendship related to the multiple im/mobilities that I study, ranging from violence imposed by international borders and immigration exclusions on Central American refugees to the violently enforced boundaries between territories of competing Salvadoran street gangs and subsequent urban fragmentation. I had come to El Salvador, in part, because of its infamy for violence. Eventually, however, I began to see how everyday marginalizations had become engraved in Gloria's diabetic body. Her life had become subtly entangled with the more sensationalist public violence of gangs and police that had been escalating in the past decade. Cecilia Menjívar (2011) and Mo Hume (2009) have examined the complex gendered interplay between structural violence, legal impunity, and public and private violence in Guatemala and El Salvador, respectively. But when Gloria and I strolled along the coast, sharing stories of bygone youth, I had not yet come to embrace a "trauma-informed research" that recognized my own life ruptures, the ruptures in the lives of others caused by my presence and my (unintended) complicities with power, and how research itself might be a mutual healing practice. In the Salvadoran context, Ariana Markowitz (2021) argues that fieldwork researchers can learn from "helping professionals" such as therapists and human-rights advocates, and this chapter takes up this dialogue.

While in El Salvador, I kept a respectful countenance, volunteering in a rural Catholic convent and conducting interviews about the violence that people experienced during their northbound journeys to the United States (Brigden 2018). But with Gloria, I relaxed. When I told a dirty joke, Gloria's cheeks would dimple with a conspiratorial smile, and she shook her hand at the wrist to say that I was naughty. We often met in the shade at the side of the road, where I would buy a Coke Zero for the long, hot bus ride to work. For a time, Gloria kept a small snack stand at the fork in the highway, where the road turned upward away from the beach and toward the small town where I had been conducting fieldwork. Across the street at the bus stop leading up the hill, another aproned woman kept a cart that sold greasy sandwiches under a worn umbrella, and they eyed each other, like gladiators across a hot asphalt battleground. Eventually, Gloria closed the shop in fear, when gang members began to demand gum, cigarettes, and money. She retreated behind the wall of her home, where her family took a loan to build a modest hostel for the surf tourists who visit the coasts of El Salvador. Her husband was well respected, and she successfully raised three dutiful boys, all in their teens and still studying when we first met. The lone sandwich woman across the street, the woman I was never destined to be friends with, held her ground.

Despite the perpetual mischief in Gloria's eyes, she suffered deeply. The loan for the hostel renovations cast a shadow over her sense of security. The sores on her swollen ankles betrayed a chronic and uncontrolled diabetic condition. Her feet often bloated uncomfortably with excess fluids, causing pain while standing; but in rural El Salvador, it is expected that middle-aged women develop "sugar in the blood." As Wendell explains, across the globe, "disability in women often goes unrecognized . . . because of the expectation that women need only be able to function well enough to perform household duties" (1996, 17). Gloria performed her duties without complaint. More than once, I wondered if anyone noticed. Indeed, I often marveled at her unmatched sharp wit in the home, but even more so, I marveled at the fact that both her husband and her sons seemed oblivious to how she outmatched them. Whatever the reason for neglect, doctors did little to make Gloria's life comfortable, her family treated her plight as unremarkable, and her neighbors seemed to do everything in their power to make her life uncomfortable. When we began a morning ritual of taking walks together, her neighbors transformed our friendship into another source of pain for Gloria. We walked alone along stretches of rocky beach, and Gloria remembered her youthful days of athleticism, when she would run shoeless along the sand and climb rocks and swim in the sea. One day, as we walked by the row of restaurants along the now-fashionable beach, a woman called out to her, "I don't know why you bother, Gloria! You will never be thin like her! You are fat!"[1] Gloria was not surprised by the verbal assault and merely acknowledged that to leave the confines of her home meant to be vulnerable to this abuse. My own "fit" body had been weaponized against hers. While she made no announcement, it was our last walk together.

After a long absence, I returned for a visit to the beach in El Salvador to rekindle old friendships. However, Gloria seemed distant. I invited her out for a girls' night, and she accepted; but after several failed attempts to collect her for the festivities, her son explained that she was no longer allowed. Whether someone disallowed it or whether Gloria simply no longer enjoyed my company remains unclear. Her son claimed that she was on some heavy cocktail of antidepressant medications and that she no longer left her house. Gloria had retreated deeper behind the walls. It was the beginning of my awareness of how gendered microviolences, embedded in diverse processes ranging from gang extortion to debt obligations to gossip to the medicalization of despair to subtle patriarchal devaluations within the home, constrain our mobility as importantly as territorial borders do. As I remembered the insults shouted by Gloria's neighbor, I also became aware of how my own white, petite, athletic body had become unwittingly implicated in boundary-making processes. I began to look for ways that my body and research could become instruments for collective healing, rather than harm.

The Bodies We Share

At the time, I could not see the true weight that Gloria carried. My own lifelong struggles with body image might be a natural starting place for research on a shared experience mediated by racial, class, ableist, and gender inequalities. These inequalities give meaning to the weight we carry on our body, though they are also often obscured by fat stigma and the blame-the-victim narratives that are so familiar in other forms of gendered violence. A rich interdisciplinary literature explores gendered body image, shaming, and fat phobias in the Global North (Bordo [1993] 2003; Boero 2013; Dworkin and Wachs 2009; Farrell 2011). In that context, Sabrina Strings (2019) convincingly traces the racist origins of Western beauty norms that prize thinness. Despite widespread anxieties about a "global obesity epidemic," the transnational medicalization of obesity, and increasing fat shaming worldwide (Brewis and Wutich 2019), few scholars have looked at how people experience these shifting corporeal constructions in daily life in countries that are less known for abundance (for a notable and exemplary exception, see Yates-Doerr 2015). As I reflected on how my own body has been weaponized and complicit in power relations in El Salvador, it became clear that white supremacy and the global apartheid system shape body image and the meaning of fat in the Global South too.

The COVID-19 pandemic laid bare the relation between health vulnerability and socioeconomic inequalities around the world, making visible the deep cleavages within societies. Related to these vulnerabilities, a slow-moving crisis of diabetes has been sweeping the globe, devastating low-income communities in particular. Thus, the global problem of hunger has become a more complex problem of nutrition, shielded from outrage by fat stigma and its fictions. While news cameras chase the yellow police tape that cordons off crime scenes and sensationalist stories of homicide, more Salvadoran women die each year from diabetes than bullets. Their deaths, while not intentional homicides, occur systematically and predictably in a country where Coca-Cola can sometimes be more accessible than clean water and where sugar plantations have long been a national mainstay. Much like the direct violence of the civil war and the subsequent street war, the twin public-health crises of poverty and diabetes must come to a reckoning with the neocolonial politics that structure them (on Belize, see Moran-Thomas 2019).

The global diabetes epidemic hit El Salvador at the same historical moment that the country experienced a massive cultural shift. While transnational migration played a role in this social transformation, so has the dramatic and rapid diffusion of cell-phone communications and social media technologies. As a consequence, a shared transnational imaginary emerged, and its messages and imagery often constitute a symbolic violence, devaluing bodies that do not conform to beauty standards embedded in existing, racial, class, and gender hierarchies. Suddenly, the "body panic" (Dworkin and Wachs 2009) and fat stigma of the Global North descended upon this corner of the Global South with renewed force. In turn, a pervasive fear of violence and economic precarity produced by neoliberal policies leads to sedentary lifestyles, limiting fitness opportunity. In this way, people feel a double burden of blame, caught between unrealistic, ableist body imagery and the political reality of contemporary El Salvador, situated at the margins of a global political economy. This is the reality that heckled Gloria on our walks together.

An encounter from many years ago illustrates how fat stigma conceals global socioeconomic injustice. On a bus ride from the coast to the capital city, I met a woman returning home after over thirty years living in Brooklyn. She was the proud mother of a US Marine, who owned a California home. Another son had a wife and children in New Jersey, and yet another attended graduate school. She was rightly proud of how far her family had come, raised on her seamstress salary: an American success story. She also told me how far her little homeland had also come, because she believed that there is no longer poverty in El Salvador. She explained it to me in English, occasionally interspersed with Spanish: "The campesinos have plenty of food. The government helps them. There are schools. But they are lazy and spend money unwisely. I see them buying bottles of soda. Many of them are fat!" I argued gently with her, but she remained adamant that "people have plenty to eat. It is not like Africa, where people starve." For her, only the image of bodies in a famine constituted the deserving poor. In her view, the fat campesinos had enough to eat and made unwise purchases, like soda, becoming responsible for their own poverty. A few minutes later, as she talked about her own expenses, she complained about how expensive food had become in El Salvador. "You can only eat pupusas cheaply! The saying is that pupusas are a gift from God, but everything is expensive here (except pupusas)." A moment after that, she explained that at least you can own a home here and you can live on next to nothing, in comparison to expensive New York. From this perspective, the fat pupusa-eating poor seemed far removed from her own struggles in an expensive faraway land where she was forced to fend for herself. Her experience of mistreatment as an immigrant in the US and her resilience in coping with that adversity seemed to have driven a wedge between her and the poor of her homeland, and in our conversation, their alleged obesity represented a visible embodiment of that barrier.

In many similar conversations, women made sense of economic inequality and their position in the global hierarchy by referencing gendered, racialized, and class-based body imagery. On the one hand, to have perceptible body fat can be a sign of status and abundance, distancing people from so-called real poverty. "Fat" can be a term of endearment in El Salvador, not necessarily an insult. In Central America, more generally, body commentary often does not imply the same judgment as it does in the United States, allowing for more matter-of-fact observations or descriptions of shape, color, or size unladen by emotion; even if people fear "obesity" as medical category, fat can be beautiful (Yates-Doerr 2015, 181). Indeed, my own athletic build is far from the stereotypical ideal. On the other hand, fat sometimes serves as an indicator of poor choices, and the images of a large female body can be evoked to set individual blame for poverty, viewed as self-imposed. Thus, even while "skinny" evokes hunger, fat stigma sometimes evokes irresponsibility, transgression, and ignorance. No matter what body women inhabit, they become caught between injurious corporeal discourses of blame and loathing (Bordo [1993] 2003). When I asked a local personal trainer about the ideal female body, he dryly replied that Salvadoran men "are enchanted by whatever woman; here they have a fat wife and a very fit lover." This attitude is not necessarily body acceptance or a worship of shapely curves or diversity of forms but instead a devaluation of women as expendable appendages to men: a different female body to suit every male need. In this sense, the pressures confronting Salvadoran women mirror the pressures that women confront in the United States and elsewhere within the contradictions of a global, capitalist beauty industry. As explained to me by a group of young women, fat women frequently hear insults from other women about their body size in the street, and women who lose weight, thereby complying with the collective criticism, often hear loud accusations of bulimia or anorexia; regardless of body type, she is likely to receive reproach from women and catcalls from men. Thus, these practices and norms are contested and complex. Nevertheless, they are disciplining and boundary-making, defining acceptable roles and spaces for gendered bodies. Indeed, body images are fundamental to how we build relationships with other bodies or how we do not.

Experiences of trauma, fat stigmatization, and the medicalization of obesity are closely linked (Gay 2017; Morgan 2020; Palmisano, Innamorati, and Vanderlinden 2016). Irena's story highlights how our bodies refract and inhabit this symbolic violence. I stayed in Irena's home while conducting research in Intipuca, El Salvador, in 2010. She was the owner of a pupusa and hamburger stand, and her son had enrolled in school to become a chef. Despite the pride that she and her son both took in their exquisite cooking abilities, her relationship to food had become fraught with anxiety, tied inexorably to a complex configuration of stressors, both past and present. The requirements of standing on her feet all day had pushed her knees into a painful refusal, and her mobility was now bound to a cane and short distances. As she talked about her struggle with her appetite and her body weight, other stories emerged: of debt and economic dislocation, her husband's physical abuse and gambling addiction, the loss of her parents to migration and then their premature death, the fragmentation of her relationships with siblings, cruelty suffered by her beloved nephew with Down syndrome, mental illness and her daughter's sexual promiscuity, spiteful gossip by neighbors that destroyed her reputation, and ultimately finding fear of Satan and solace in God. She began to eat as a form of self-harm. In desperation and loss, she had seriously considered killing herself and poisoning her two children, but God forgives. As she framed these stories, she often juxtaposed my lithe body with hers, reminding me of how fortunate I am by complimenting how thin I remain despite gobbling down multiple servings of her deliciously prepared food. Our different body shapes seemed to contain our divergent fates, and the frequent comparisons, often with an undertone of self-loathing that I hear often from other women on my travels, made me entirely uneasy. However, in moments of greater levity than our meals, Irena and I would attempt to Zumba together in front of her television, laughing at our shared ineptitude in the dance routines.

Bodies and Worlds Drifting Apart

Unlike those difficult meals with Irena, Fatima and I had an easy coffee, catching up after my pandemic-imposed absence from El Salvador. As we talked about Fatima's own fitness habits, our conversation veered to why Fatima quit her primary athletic hobby. She quit running after a man assaulted her during a morning jog. In what constitutes a mundane occurrence, he had slapped her hard on the ass as he rode by on a bicycle, and she had cried tears of anger and frustration. In contrast to Fatima's experience, joggers routinely circle the US embassy compound, finding a sense of security under its surveillance. Disciplining practices associated with class and gender, refracted in this instance through the geopolitical presence of a neoimperial outpost within an urban landscape, shape our access to fitness. So I asked Fatima about these women, often scantily clad in sports bras and Lycra that would attract an obscene amount of attention in working-class neighborhoods. Fatima's explanation of the relative safety for jogging in the rich areas near the embassy seamlessly strayed into talking about the pandemic quarantine's limits on working-class mobility. She pointed out that the quarantine had been strictly enforced where she lived in Zacamil, as soldiers and police descended on the neighborhood to whisk violators away to concentration centers, but she imagined that a similar siege did not occur in wealthy parts of the city.

In response, I asked about the impact of the quarantine on the working-class women whom Fatima works with through a nonprofit outreach. She explained that incapable of selling in the streets and carrying their goods over their head to market, the women had no physical activity at all. Under four months of stay-at-home orders, the women also experienced terrible food insecurity, relying exclusively on the inadequate nutritional supplies donated by the government. In a moment of levity, Fatima laughed remembering what her teammate Maria told the women after seeing them again, concerned about donors' willingness to give charity, "Nobody is going to believe that they are in poverty, because they aren't undernourished. . . . They are just malnourished. Because all of them were fatties. All! But it was because of this, . . . because the food [insecurity]." While our conversation was lighthearted and Maria's comments were meant to be a gentle ribbing among friends all sharing the same struggle with their weight, a bit of dry camaraderie, I wondered aloud what suffering simmered underneath the good humor. I asked Fatima if she thought they felt good about their bodies. The answer was an unequivocal "no." All of the women reported the worsening of various health conditions, and two of them needed emergency funds for x-rays because of debilitating back pain.

Indeed, the COVID-19 quarantine had a deleterious impact on the well-being of working-class urban women in El Salvador, compounding preexisting trauma and illnesses. In this moment, interpersonal and familial violence at home also intensified dramatically. Thus, Silvia Federici's writing seems prophetic: "Beside the danger of medical speculation and malpractice, there is the further concern that body remakes remain individual solutions and add to the process of social stratification and exclusion as the 'care of the body' requires more money, time and access to services and resources than the majority can afford. . . . While some bodies are becoming more fit, more perfect, the number of those who can hardly move because of excess weight, illness and poor nutrition is growing. Bodies and worlds are drifting apart" (2020, 55). When I shared these thoughts with a group of working-class women, they immediately connected their fitness challenges to a context of state impunity, endemic intimate partner violence, and gang and police predation. To understand their analysis of these connections at a deeper level, as well as to respond to their immediate needs, I am developing research to grow our worlds back together by healing our relationship with our bodies.

Research as Healing

To conduct research on embodiment, we formed a nascent research partnership between a nonprofit that I founded, called Pesas y Poder, and a women's empowerment nonprofit in El Salvador, called Programa Velasco. As a team, we ask Salvadoran women how they feel, think, move, describe, and see their bodies before, during, and after a series of movement workshops. We analyze how body and identity respond to structural violence and everyday trauma, tracing the relationship between our gendered sense of corporeal self and the inequities of urban life. The physical containment of the quarantine multiplied and threw in stark relief these inequities. By simultaneously exploring how violence is worn in the body and also promoting empathy for our own bodies and those of others, it is trauma-informed research.

The danger of this research lies in its potential to reinforce corporeal discipline and fat stigma, rather than to become a liberatory practice. Whether conducting research in El Salvador or the United States, participants bring their own purpose to these projects, often informed by preconceived ideas about the health value of weight loss and mainstream notions of feminine beauty. As women, we carry our trauma in our movements, posture, and breathing patterns, as well as our motivation. Participants may enter the program not primarily to explore the embodiment of their trauma or resist power structures but instead to achieve aesthetic goals; this mismatch of aims signals a fundamental tension between the goals of body acceptance and body transformation, which may be difficult to reconcile in activities coded as "fitness" or a space recognized as a "gym." By encouraging physical practice, the research could become an additional source of shaming for nonconforming bodies. This danger is compounded by my own leadership, as a foreign, white, athletic, cis-presenting woman. To navigate this danger, women will engage in a feminist collaboration to design an embodied empowerment program for others in similar situations. This design self-consciously harnesses empathy and our own body intuitions to strive toward solidarity. Grounded in participatory action research (PAR), this work builds on interdisciplinary literatures from fat studies, recent innovations in trauma-informed yoga and weightlifting, and feminist methodologies, which together suggest the importance of somatic approaches to both research and healing.[2]

The concept of trauma provides a focal point for grounded exploration of the complex coconstruction and sociospatial interweaving ("intercorporeality") of body, mind, and lived environ to which feminist scholars of embodiment have long called our attention (e.g., Grosz 1994; Price and Shildrick 1999; Young 2005; Weiss 1999). The body carries our oppression in its neurological system, physical mannerisms, and patterns of social interaction, sometimes passed down over generations in a community (Haines 2019; Menakem 2019). This trauma can be deeply internalized, held subconsciously in muscle memory rather than surfacing in narrative form (Van der Kolk 2014). By definition, trauma ruptures the self, undermining a sense of autonomy and security (Herman 1992). In the aftermath of this rupture, survivors often experience emotional and sensory dissociations that preclude possibilities of trust, both in their own body and in other people (Herman 1992). Prolonged adversity can rewire the human body, altering its hormonal signaling and internal messaging with epigenetic impact (Harris 2018). The mechanisms underpinning these responses are simultaneously biological, cultural, and psychological.

Within this integrated mind/body approach to understanding the impact of violence, research workshops use bodywork, including strength training and calisthenics, to break cognitive scripts and pose new questions for participants. Guided physical activities and community building exercises can literally move us beyond narrative and into touch, posture, spatial awareness, balance, and breathing to challenge ingrained modes of being in the body. In the process, we make discoveries about our experience of violence, how it shapes our body, our patterns of movement, and our relation with others. We become physically grounded. As a collective, we will also explore the double entendre of words like "resistance," "power," "mobility," and "performance," which carry meaning in both athletic and political worlds. In addition to these group exercises, a small cohort of women will be asked to perform, in the privacy of their own home, gentle strengthening movements, provided in a video format. Then, at the offices of the local nonprofit, they will privately report changes in their sensations, attitudes, perception, and understanding of their body and the bodies of others over time at a listening kiosk station. The women will also provide feedback to design actionable plans for self-care for other women in their social setting, and we will ask women to draw connections between their exercises and their usual work and household tasks, encouraging them to identify hidden forms of athleticism in their daily lives. Ultimately, participants will be offered the opportunity to critique the program, altering the design to facilitate discoveries for future cohorts.

The research aims of this initial project, which is still in the preparation phase, are (1) to describe the experience of quarantine for urban Salvadoran women; (2) to understand the relationship between this experience and intersecting oppressions of class and gender that structure their daily lives; (3) to design an embodied empowerment program specific to the cultural understandings, needs, and resources available to these women during and after the COVID-19 crisis; and (4) to understand when and how gentle, daily movement can change sensations, attitudes, perceptions, and narratives of the self and others, thereby creating opportunities for resilience and resistance to structural violence. This research self-consciously blurs the boundary between research and healing. Strength training fosters resilience, increases a sense of agency, practices healthy nervous-system responses, and facilitates positive relational connections to self and others (Whitworth et al. 2017, 2019). High-intensity and functional movements may offer special benefits for coping with trauma (Mastrorillo 2020). A key step for trauma survivors is the reestablishment of a sense of autonomy and control, followed by social reconnection and recognition of our mutual interdependence (Herman 1992). Encouraging survivors to take ownership of research and program development fosters this recentering of self. Encouraging survivors to create community in that process, building empathy for how others inhabit their own bodies, fosters the recentering of solidarity. Thus, I hope to practice "trauma-informed research methods" to explore how spectacular and mundane violences intersect within our bodies.

Trauma provides a conceptual tool for locating struggle and social fragmentation in the body. Following Wendell (1996) and an ethics developed by feminist scholars of disability, this project emphasizes the quest to live within our bodies' limitations, rather than to transform their shape, eliminate weakness, or transcend suffering. In that sense, athletic performances and fitness rituals can serve an unconventional purpose; the goal is an awareness of the intersectional oppressions that shape the body. We thereby encourage self-compassion and collective confrontation of those injustices. As Federici explains, "our struggle then must begin with a reappropriation of our body, the revaluation and rediscovery of its capacity for resistance, and expansion and celebration of its powers, individual and collective" (2020, 123). To celebrate these powers, we also need to embrace our bodily imperfections and pain, experiencing and contextualizing our corporeal limits (Wendell 1996). Answering this call for embodied discernment, research becomes healing and care work. In this way, the convergence of feminist theories of the body and somatic-healing practices promises a timely intervention on both our knowledge and experience of multiple, intersecting gendered violences.

NOTES

1. This is paraphrased from memory, and Gloria is a pseudonym (as are all names in this chapter). Other stories have been pulled from field notes.
2. This nascent research also builds on a proposed team collaboration called Restorative Justice in Movement, which focuses on trauma and transformation for women from communities that are disproportionately impacted by mass incarceration in Milwaukee.

REFERENCES

Boero, Natalie. 2013. *Killer Fat: Media, Medicine and Morals in the American Obesity Epidemic*. New Brunswick, NJ: Rutgers University Press.

Bordo, Susan. (1993) 2003. *Unbearable Weight: Feminism, Wester Culture, and the Body*. 10th anniversary ed. Berkeley: University of California Press.

Brewis, Alexandra, and Amber Wutich. 2019. *Lazy, Crazy, and Disgusting: Stigma and the Undoing of Global Health*. Baltimore: Johns Hopkins University Press.

Brigden, Noelle. 2018. *The Migrant Passage: Clandestine Journeys from Central America*. Ithaca, NY: Cornell University Press.

———. 2021. "From La Monjita to La Hormiga: Reflections on Gender, Body and Power in Fieldwork." *Geopolitics* 6 (1): 118–38.

Dworkin, Shari L., and Faye Linda Wachs. 2009. *Body Panic: Gender, Health, and the Selling of Fitness*. New York: New York University Press.

Farrell, Amy Erdman. 2011. *Fat Shame: Stigma and the Fat Body in American Culture*. New York: New York University Press.

Federici, Silvia. 2020. *Beyond the Periphery of the Skin: Rethinking, Remaking and Reclaiming the Body in Contemporary Capitalism*. Oakland, CA: Kairos.

Gay, Roxane. 2017. *Hunger: A Memoir of (My) Body*. New York: Harper.

Grosz, Elizabeth. 1994. *Volatile Bodies: Toward a Corporeal Feminism*. Bloomington: Indiana University Press.

Haines, Staci K. 2019. *The Politics of Trauma: Somatics, Healing and Social Justice*. Berkeley, CA: North Atlantic Books.

Harris, Nadine Burke. 2018. *The Deepest Well: Healing the Long-Term Effects of Childhood Adversity*. Boston: Mariner Books.

Herman, Judith. 1992. *Trauma and Recovery: The Aftermath of Violence from Domestic Abuse to Political Terror*. New York: Basic Books.

Hume, Mo. 2009. *The Politics of Violence: Gender, Conflict and Community in El Salvador*. New York: Wiley.

Markowitz, Ariana. 2021. "The Better to Break and Bleed With: Research, Violence and Trauma." *Geopolitics* 26 (1): 94–117.

Mastrorillo, Alessia. 2020. "Between my Breaths: CrossFit as an Embodied Healing Practice in North America." Unpublished manuscript.

Menakem, Rasmaa. 2019. *My Grandmother's Hands: Racialized Trauma and the Pathway to Mending our Hearts and Bodies*. Las Vegas: Central Recovery.

Menjívar, Cecilia. 2011. *Enduring Violence: Latina Women's Lives in Guatemala*. Berkeley: University of California Press.

Messner, Michael A. 2018. "Gender Relations and Sport: Local, National, Transnational." *No Slam Dunk: Gender, Sport and the Unevenness of Social Change*, edited by Cheryl Cooky and Michael A. Messner, 54–69. New Brunswick, NJ: Rutgers University Press.

Moran-Thomas, Amy. 2019. *Traveling with Sugar: Chronicles of a Global Epidemic*. Berkeley: University of California Press.

Morgan, Eleanor. 2020. "Obesity Can't Be Tackled until We Address the Trauma That Causes It." *The Guardian*, July 30, 2020. www.theguardian.com.

Palmisano, Giovanni Luca, Marco Innamorati, and Johan Vanderlinden. 2016. "Life Adverse Experiences in Relation with Obesity and Binge Eating Disorder." *Journal of Behavioral Addiction* 5 (1): 11–31.

Price, Janet, and Margrit Shildrick. 1999. *Feminist Theory and the Body: A Reader*. New York: Routledge.

Strings, Sabrina. 2019. *Fearing the Black Body: The Racial Origins of Fat Phobia*. New York: New York University Press.

Van der Kolk, Bessel. 2014. *The Body Keeps the Score: Brain, Mind, and Body in the Healing of Trauma*. New York: Penguin Books.

Wendell, Susan. 1996. *The Rejected Body: Feminist Philosophical Reflections on Disability*. New York: Routledge.

Weiss, Gail. 1999. *Body Images: Embodiment as Intercorporeality*. New York: Routledge.

Whitmarsh, Ian. 2013. "The Ascetic Subject of Compliance: The Turn to Chronic Diseases in Global Health." In *When People Come First: Critical Studies in Global Health*, edited by Joao Biehl and Adriana Petryna, 302–34. Princeton, NJ: Princeton University Press.

Whitworth, James W., Lynette L. Craft, Shira I. Dunsiger, and Joseph T. Ciccolo. 2017. "Direct and Indirect Effect of Exercise on Post-Traumatic Stress Disorder Symptoms: A Longitudinal Study." *General Hospital Psychology* 49:56–62.

Whitworth, James W., Sanaz Nosrat, Nicholas J. SantaBarbara, and Joseph T. Ciccolo. 2019. "Feasibility of Resistance Exercise for Post-Traumatic Stress and Anxiety Symptoms: A Randomized Controlled Pilot Study." *Journal of Traumatic Stress* 32 (6): 977–84.

Yates-Doerr, Emily. 2015. *The Weight of Obesity: Hunger and Global Health in Postwar Guatemala*. Berkeley: University of California Press.

Young, Iris Marion. 2005. *On Female Body Experience: Throwing like a Girl and Other Essays*. Oxford: Oxford University Press.

10

Intersectionality in the Courts

Collaborative Feminist Ethnography of Sexual Assault Adjudication

AMBER JOY POWELL, SAMEENA MULLA, AND
HEATHER R. HLAVKA

Interpellating Adjudicants and Researchers

A young Black man with braids and long sideburns, dressed in the gray tee-shirt and orange pants worn by many in-custody defendants, entered the courtroom. After taking a moment to speak with his lawyer, his sentencing hearing began. He was twelve years old when he pled to a sexual offense charge and was required to register as a sex offender for at least fifteen years. At this sentencing, he was charged with violating the conditions of his probation, in addition to marijuana possession and bail jumping. The white public defender requested leniency: his client was just trying to support his family yet chose "stupid" ways to make money. The white judge did not see it that way: "You had a child out of wedlock who you can't support. Get a job! Get an education!" He blamed the young man for contributing to "another child growing up in the community without a father," suggesting that he simply "keep it in his pants."

This was a typical scene in the Milwaukee County courts, where we conducted our field research. At this point in our observations, we found the judge's offensive admonishment neither shocking nor unusual. Our ethnographic observations on sexual assault adjudication revealed that these racial degradation ceremonies (Gonzalez Van Cleve 2016) were routine for Black and Latino adjudicants. For two years, we witnessed judges, attorneys, and deputies berate litigants—mocking their speech,

chastising their family members for breaking minor courtroom proto-
cols, and routinely calling defendants everything from "hood rats" to
"sadistic, evil, monsters." Black and Latina women were also subjugated
through routine mispronunciations of their names, commentary about
their "unprofessional" attire, misgendering (in the case of transwomen),
and attempts to discredit their testimonies by characterizing them as
"liars," drug users, and sex workers. Even jurors became the targets of
suspicion when attorneys and judges openly pried into their sexual
abuse histories.

We understood that the criminal prosecution of sexual violence was
(and remains) deeply invested in racial hierarchies, class identity, and
cultural commitments to normative understandings of gender and
sexuality that exploit both litigants and their communities (Flood 2012;
Gonzalez Van Cleve 2016; Sommerville 2005). Yet, in documenting
these experiences, we became aware that our own racialized, gendered,
classed, and aged identities as white, South Asian American, and Black
women were also crucial in understanding the court as a site of gendered, racialized violence. People perceived us each as "belonging" to
the courthouse in different ways: as court personnel, lawyers, litigants,
or family members. Varying perceptions of who we were and assumptions of why we were in the courthouse exposed both the explicit and
subtle forms of racial, sexual, and gender politics that subjected public
bodies—including our own—to suspicion, harassment, and violence in
the courts. Ruha Benjamin's analysis of the carceral imagination asks,
"Who and what are fixed in place—classified, corralled, and/or coerced,
to enable innovation?" (2016, 150). Through the process of interrogating
how the courts operated to fix us and other courtroom denizens in place,
we focused on how an embodied methodology could vividly reveal the
court's investments in racial, gender, sexual, and class hierarchies.

In this chapter, we chronicle three aspects of our ethnographic project
observing sexual assault adjudication. First, we articulate the way we
developed our feminist collaboration by centering intersectionality and
embodiment in our method. Then we confront the courthouse's racial,
gender, sexual, and class politics as an embodied experience. Finally, we
detail how we cultivated writing practices that captured various intersectional vulnerabilities in the court context, including our own. Our
epistemological and methodological analysis broadens previous ap-

proaches to gender-based violence research in two ways. First, we argue that our own interpellation into courthouse hierarchies yielded insight into how these processes might entangle and subjectivate the vulnerable subjects.[1] The court's processes of interpellation, its enactment of power and domination sustained by criminal prosecution, had uneven purchase, among both participants and ourselves. While the forms of interpellation and subjectivation of the research team were often relatively low stakes, these everyday occurrences operated in continuity with the more conscripting forms of surveillance and domination characteristic of sexual assault adjudication, particularly in the surveillance of Blackness (Browne 2015).

Second, we engage with intersectionality as a critical social theory of power relations (Collins 2019) that structures courtroom interactions. Patricia Hill Collins argues that critical intersectional engagement exceeds a simple analysis of interlocking identities: instead, intersectionality's "critical inquiry taps the recursive relationship of knowledge and power as organized via epistemology and methodology" (2019, 136). Within the context of collaboration, this meant valorizing our collective standpoints in the courts as legitimate ways of knowing, disrupting epistemic traditions that posit courts, jails, and prisons as "justice" for victims, and forging political commitments toward anticarceral feminist praxis that builds "a society where it is possible to address harm without relying on structural forms of oppression or the violent systems that increase it" (Kaba 2021, 3; Clair and Woog 2022).

Cultivating Feminist Collaboration and Method

Feminist collaborations take time and must be built with intention. Sameena and Heather both have long histories working with survivors of sexual violence, engaging community advocacy and activism, and researching sexual assault. Our shared history around gender-based violence work led to a multidisciplinary, collaborative project about sexual assault. Drawing on feminist theory, anthropology, sociology, and criminology created a unique space for us to engage in different training histories, theories, methodologies, and writing styles. While Sameena primarily focused on developing ethnographic field techniques and feminist theory, exemplified in her first book on rape crisis interventions (Mulla 2014), Heather broadly trained as a sociologist specializing in qualitative method and had cultivated a nuanced approach to discourse and narrative analysis in her work on child forensic interviews (Hlavka 2010, 2013, 2014, 2017, 2019). After meeting in 2008, Sameena and Heather sought to incorporate each other's methodologies into a single project that spanned several years.

Before intensive fieldwork began, Sameena and Heather invited several undergraduate students to participate in the project. Given the project's sensitive nature, each undergraduate student met with the faculty researchers individually, was trained in method, ethics, and the subject area of sexual violence, and was included in group meetings, where we intentionally and collectively prepared for the emotional challenges of observing sexual assault hearings. We encouraged our students to document emotionally compelling issues in their field notes, allowing them to develop their own notation styles. Our approach was rooted in the feminist suspicion of the separation between emotion and reason (Jaggar 1989), centering intellection, an approach that associates feeling with a form of knowing and does not seek to privilege some sensory modalities of attention while diminishing others (Mulla 2017; Smith 1998). In practice, this meant that we kept meticulous notes of interactions that deeply unsettled us and returned to these episodes for more pointed and intensive analysis and theorization.

As our fieldwork outings hit a stride, we made sure that all of the research team maintained lines of communication should anyone need to debrief. Weekly emails and daily text messages became ways to monitor these phenomena as they emerged. While we wrote our field notes individually, we were sensitized collectively by sharing these experiences. Situated on different sides of a large courtroom, if not in different courtrooms altogether, we frequently alerted one another to these charged moments. Our text-messaging log became another document we compiled and relied on as part of our field notes. We sent text messages surreptitiously from within the courtroom, or we exited to the hallways and restrooms during breaks because the use of cell phones was prohibited in the gallery. Here, we understood that we were not subject to the same level of disciplinary action as other public occupants. Only once during our fieldwork did one of us forget to silence our cell-phone ringer, and when it rang in court, Heather found herself mortified and rushed out of the courtroom. The sheriff's deputies laughed about the incident and brushed it off, teasing her on later occasions. Heather had witnessed others being disciplined in a harsh manner for making the same mistake, revealing how court might interpellate her into its hierarchy.

Confronting Racial, Gendered, and Sexual Courthouse Politics

We were not in the courts for very long before we began to experience the daily indignities of the court's power. By the middle of the summer in 2013, we had incorporated ourselves into the courtroom flow, where our race, gender, perceived class status, and attire continued to shape how we were treated. Heather and Sameena were routinely outfitted in the professional uniforms of academic women and, as such, were often mistaken for social workers, victim advocates, or attorneys. The security staff frequently commented that Heather and Sameena should ask the chief judge for a pass to skip the security line. In contrast, some attorneys and deputies asked Amber if she was there to see one of the Black defendants, assuming that she was a supportive girlfriend or sister. Most times, and perhaps because of Amber's casual appearance, large backpack, notebook, and pens, courthouse staff often asked her if she was a high school or college student. Neither Heather nor Sameena were to their knowledge ever associated with defendants, and Amber did not experience the reprimands often directed toward other Black women in the courtroom gallery.

Race and racial hierarchy infuse the space of the Milwaukee County courts in remarkably unsubtle ways. While crime statistics and survey data demonstrate that sexual violence is largely intraracial (Morgan and Truman 2020, 19) and common across all racial groups, Milwaukee sexual assault adjudication disproportionately involved victims, witnesses, and defendants who were people of color. Black and Brown observers filled the gallery, while the people behind the bullet-proof glass separating the gallery from the courtroom staff were mostly white. As we moved through the courts and observed others' movements, we recorded how bodies were differentially disciplined. We waved or nodded our heads at the deputies when entering the courtrooms, while others were stopped, questioned, and directed to designated areas. As mediators of potential gallery conflict, deputies enforced spatial separations between parties supporting the defense or prosecution. Only we were free to switch sides during hearings. As we took empty gallery seats, some people tried to figure out who we were and what we were writing in our notebooks. Perhaps they thought we were *Milwaukee Journal Sentinel* legal affairs journalists, sometimes stationed in highly publicized court hearings. Though most stared out of curiosity, some expressed discomfort and perhaps discontent with our presence. We tried to be more sensitive to when and where we wrote our field notes, pausing when family members became visibly upset during hearings. On multiple occasions, family members of defendants and victims came to recognize us as regular court attendees who might have information on judges, attorneys, and case schedules. Families and their friends often preferred to ask us about scheduling rather than subject themselves to potential hostility from courtroom deputies.

Occasionally, we chatted with attorneys, deputies, and even judges with whom we had become familiar. During these informal talks, we learned new details about cases. For example, after a very upsetting case involving a defendant who had impregnated his daughter, a deputy told Amber that the victim's baby was still in the hospital suffering from several physical health problems. He further gossiped that the defendant's reaction to his daughter's pregnancy was, "I knew I should have put her on birth control!" During the sentencing hearing itself, the judge labeled the defendant a monster, chiding him for the child that would now become "a burden on the system." During the judge's graphic description, we observed the victim leaving the courtroom, blotting tears from her eyes. Deputies, and even attorneys, operated under the assumption that as researchers, we wanted to hear these lurid, oftentimes graphic details. And while acquiring this "backstage" information may have been productive data collection, it increased the emotional toll of daily exposure to narratives of violence. At times, Amber felt that she was being initiated into a circle of confidence in which she did not wish to participate. This circle of confidence was sometimes evident to the public as well. During one lunch hour, a judge motioned for Heather and Sameena to join him in the gallery. At the same time, the deputies began escorting several handcuffed and ankle-chained defendants back to the jail. The judge commented, "These guys really don't like me." As they were marched out of the courtroom, "these guys" eyed the judge and researchers, some with curiosity, others with hostility. Afterward, Heather and Sameena discussed their sense of discomfort being associated with the judge. His extension of the court's racial hierarchy was another moment in which we saw ourselves interpellated into the court's practices of racial domination.

Our emotions and affective embodiment were yet another way in which we were all fixed in place by the court. Comments from the judges condemning Black families hit each member of the research team in different ways. Born and raised in Milwaukee, Amber was deeply personally connected and committed to its places, people, and communities. It was not uncommon for her to recognize names and faces, and we all recognized a jury member or two. These moments of recognition challenged the myth of the detached observer.

During one sentencing hearing, an exasperated judge commented, "This is another case where this community is so far gone. I've got to leave. I've got to move to Montana or somewhere else. The behavior in this community is so uncivilized, it's unbelievable." The judge then turned to the young Black defendant, and queried, "I hate to ask, because I'm not going to like the answer: Do you have a father in your life?" While Blackness was not explicitly indexed, all present understood that the judge was singling out Milwaukee's Black community. The judge's selection of "Montana," offered as a contrasting haven to which the judge wished to flee, was conspicuous in its whiteness.[2] The frequent invocation of failed Black fatherhood was another regular feature of sentencing hearings. Eventually, we began to anticipate when Black fatherhood and Black families would be scrutinized during a trial or sentencing hearing. Such statements, routinely and unselfconsciously stated in open court, offered insights into the court's perception of communities and local geographies. It also signaled to us that the judge, and the courtroom staff overall, presumed that the research team might share these sentiments. Again, the court either made assumptions about our alignments and relationships or dismissed them as inconsequential.

With toddlers at home, Sameena and Heather often found the court's pronouncements on the inadequacy of motherhood grating, aware of the undue scrutiny on Black mothers. As the sentencing hearing continued, the judge emphasized to the defendant, "Your father should have kicked your butt from one end of Milwaukee County to the other and then locked you in the basement. . . . And since your father is not around, your mother should have done the same thing." Mother blame was a repetitive motif in the courts (Powell, Hlavka, and Mulla 2017). It was not possible, or desirable, to hear these utterances, watch the pained expressions of the people around us gritting their teeth, muttering under their breath, or walking out of the courtroom because they could not bear the continued diatribe, without feeling these things ourselves. Those family and friends who did not hide their emotions were often spoken to sharply, escorted out of the court, or even cited for contempt.

Our own bodies were included in the display and spectacle of bodies in the courthouse, from the security lines to the daily marching of imprisoned defendants in and out of the courtrooms. In the courthouse, official surveillance also paralleled the sexual surveillance of the streets. As a public venue, the courthouse was a space for (mostly) men to comment on others' appearances. Many Black and Brown women in the courthouse, including Amber and Sameena, were subjected to these forms of harassment (Hanson and Richards 2019). They experienced men asking for their phone numbers or commenting on their bodies in the staircases, security lines, hallways, and even the courtroom galleries. Men put their own cell phones in their pockets and asked to borrow Amber's or Sameena's or hissed and catcalled in the hallways. As many women do in their everyday lives, Amber and Sameena tried to find humor in these incidents, to ignore them, or to simply bear them. We recorded instances of the security guards who were too "thirsty" or "creepy" and unwanted behavior from men in the galleries. These interactions highlight assumptions about access to women's bodies—especially women of color, who bore the brunt of men's sexual harassment.

Where unwanted sexual attention might manifest itself at any moment, there was great vulnerability for all women who passed through the security checkpoint. Security guards searched, scanned, commented on, and at times even touched women's bodies. It was not uncommon for security guards to ask women, "Was that a bra wire? Lift up your shirt, show your waist. Remove your shoes. Take everything out of your pockets." It became well-known that many of the security guards were "handsy." Such comments simultaneously marked protection with humor, communicating to team members which guards were likely to "linger a bit too long" with the security wand and which guards routinely requested that one lift up their shirt to see their waist. One morning a familiar guard greeted Heather and Sameena with a smile, asking, "You ladies again?" Sameena moved through the checkpoint and waited for Heather (Hlavka and Mulla 2021, 33). As the guard placed Heather's bag on a belt for screening, he told her to step aside so he could check her with the security wand. He then grabbed Heather's waist and firmly slid his hands up and down her rib cage, brushing against her breast. The invasive touch made Heather freeze. She felt trapped, unable to move. She wanted to yell, "What the hell are you doing?" Stunned and disoriented, she remained silent as she fumbled to collect the remainder of her belongings from the x-ray machine. It was not until they climbed the first floor of stairs that she told Sameena. Court had started, but Sameena ushered Heather to a hallway bench to take a break, to breathe, and to talk. This incident was a painful reminder of the ease with which sexual violence inserts itself into women's routine worlds, in semipublic spaces and within earshot of allies and friends. We understood that, as a research team, we were not exempt from the forms of sexual power exerted by men in the courtroom, particularly men in uniform. We worried about the other women entering court who were even more vulnerable to these forced attentions and unwanted touches, while strategizing how to keep ourselves safe. We shared the experience and warned team members about the security guard, avoiding this courthouse checkpoint for some time afterward.

Although we, as feminist scholars, had not started from a position in which we imagined being a detached, "objective," or disinterested observer, these interactions disrupted any fiction that we could transcend our own gendered, racialized, and sexualized flesh while conducting this project. At the checkpoints, in the hallways, and in the courtroom, the court asserted its theories and operations of power on every single person who passed through its systems. Conveying these power dynamics through our writing was one more challenge we took on as a collaborative research team.

Writing Embodied Experiences

M. Gabriela Torres (2019) writes that feminist anthropology centers on building and maintaining meaningful relationships as a mechanism to

challenge entrenched patriarchal and capitalist ideas of knowledge production. Coauthorship, Torres argues, brings to light how dialogue and
teamwork are foundational to knowledge acquisition and production.
For us, coauthorship began long before we immersed ourselves in the
thousands of field notes, transcripts, memos, and writings. This mutually produced ethnographic record was shaped by our frequent texts,
phone calls, emails, hallway conversations, and debriefing during lunch
breaks. Discussions of our visceral reactions to fieldwork and its impact
on our lives were inscribed in our work. Because of this methodological
work, we could collect and examine those moments in which we were
conscious of the ways the court sought to interpellate us into its hierarchies and forms of racial ordering and domination.

Coauthorship also requires trust and generates forms of accountability and vulnerability that require continued investment in collaborative
relationships. The courts were not the only institutions into which we
were interpellated. As researchers, we faced pressures of academic pub-
lishing, graduate school applications, and tenure clocks. But we were
also teachers, students, partners, mothers, daughters, caretakers, and
survivors. Respecting our roles, identities, and responsibilities outside
the research context meant consciously resisting institutional pressures
to go by a single clock. Doing so prolonged the writing process and extended professional milestones, but this commitment was necessary to
allow each contributor an opportunity to shape our writing projects.
Recognizing that we held simultaneous obligations was a crucial part
of maintaining strong feminist collaboration. Writing together revealed
our own vulnerabilities and insecurities, and we made these explicit for
one another. As feminist ethnographers, we were well versed in writing
about the lived experiences of power and privilege, yet incorporating
ourselves and our bodies into these narratives remained difficult. With
little formal training on reflexive practices, both Heather and Amber
found it "strange" to write about oneself in an academic article. Despite
the growing recognition that intersectionality is a significant theory of
power (Collins 2019), Heather's and Sameena's academic training included few spaces for engaging intersectionality within their own research areas. In many instances, academic writing that appeared too
close, too invested, or too political faced critique—particularly in criminology and sociology—that such accounts of social life were not "sci-

entific enough." Initially, Sameena's own training as an anthropologist made her dismissive of the notion that ethnographic research should aspire to be scientific. Recognizing that our work would be read across an interdisciplinary field of scholars, Sameena, Heather, and Amber learned to address these critiques together. Together, we produced a style of writing that took seriously the tensions in our disciplinary approaches and our joint feminist commitments.

Our time away from active data collection allowed us to revisit it from a new, more critical perspective. Fieldwork wound down as Black Lives Matter organizers took to the streets, calling for justice across the country. Witnessing the murders of Black and Brown men, women, and trans people at the hands of the carceral state challenged any remaining commitments we had to criminal justice reform. These painful moments strengthened our investment in abolition by forcing us to acknowledge that courts—like police, prisons, jails, probation, or parole—rarely serve as sites of rehabilitation or justice for anyone (Gonzalez Van Cleve 2016). We began to explore and adopt the position that abolition was and is a legitimate, necessary tool to address gender-based violence in ways that do not reproduce racial trauma (Kaba 2021; Kim 2018).

Heeding the lessons of Black feminist scholars and activists, we strove to avoid reproducing epistemic violence through the exclusion of Black, Brown, queer, and trans women's experiences of sexual violence in feminist projects (Brown and Jones 2018; Kaba 2021). Prior anti-rape-movement feminist accounts largely avoided the racialization of rape, which unduly targets young Black and Brown men as culprits of sexual assault and reinforces state reliance on criminalization as an effective response to gender-based violence (Richie 2012). In acknowledging this history, we reflected on how to do justice in our descriptions of violence against Black and Brown women and children without reifying the racialized cultural tropes of Black and Brown men as "mopes and monsters" (Gonzalez Van Cleve 2016). How could the act of writing this ethnography hold accountable the interlocking power structures and carceral logics that produce vulnerabilities to sexual violence without giving way to the abjection of the defendant? Heather and Sameena's book includes a chapter focused on defendants and the oft-repeated trope of inadequate fatherhood that we wrote about earlier in this chapter (Hlavka and Mulla 2021, 213). In thinking explicitly about the conventions of the court, we sought to produce a style of writing that consciously departed from the conventions we had all observed in the court.

Because the courts were replete with the spectacle of women's suffering, as a writing practice, we audited every description of violence in our published work. Was this detail necessary to include? Where testimony had been compelled in the courts, should we reproduce in the text what was unwillingly offered? Where we could, we often opted for decentering descriptions of acts of sexual assault, including fewer details and shifting our emphasis to the suffering that was caused by participation in the process of adjudication itself. Rather than emphasizing what had happened to a person's body, we drew attention to the way they were compelled to narrate their experiences, including affect, gestures, and thus the embodiment of suffering. Our writing standard, once again, was to make clear the court's power and to describe sexual assault adjudication without making the court's stance our own. Reflecting on our written words, we knew that we could never be certain whether we had always made the right choice. We held each other accountable and listened when one collaborator suggested a different word or made a retraction. Collectively, we take responsibility for the choices we have made.

Conclusion

This chapter has drawn on the distinctive experiences of our research team to show how collaborative methodologies can strengthen research on sexual assault adjudication. Collaborative work must be intentionally facilitated and sustained. Our work centers reflexive intersectional methods to draw attention to processes of interpellation and the production of power relations (Collins 2019). The legal analysis of intersectionality put forward by Kimberlé Crenshaw in "Mapping the Margins" (1991) is specifically about the vulnerability of women of color navigating the criminal justice system as victims of gender-based violence. In developing our collaborative field-research method, we returned to intersectionality as Crenshaw had developed it through the particular site of gender violence and criminal justice institutions. To identify the work of power within episodes we experienced in the field, we prioritized emotion, making note of our discomfort and allowing it to be generative. We were attuned to our bodies and our affect and how intersectionality inflected both. Finally, we offered insights into collaborative writing processes that can hold ethnographers accountable for mirroring and reproducing the violence of the courts. We maintain that our feminist methodologies, which value the embodiment of knowledge, produce a more rigorous and nuanced analysis, one that must be reproduced in scholarly practices. If institutions do not provide space or incentive to nurture collaborative approaches, particularly those practiced by multiracial, multidisciplinary, and multigenerational research teams, both the health of the researchers and the quality of knowledge are at stake.

Returning to the opening scene of a sentencing hearing with which we began this chapter, the young man before the court was subjected to humiliation and domination through the judge's proclamation that the defendant should "put it in his pants." The judge's disgust existed alongside his power to imprison this young Black man for participating in a drug crime that was in violation of the rules of the sex-offender registry. Although the charge was related to drugs, the judge saw fit to comment on the sexual behavior of the young man before the court. Such proclamations drove the public spectacle of sexual assault adjudication, and as witnesses to the scene, we were also interpellated into the court's racial hierarchy. The judge's voicing of this hierarchy was accompanied by the embodiment of this hierarchy. The young man had been immediately taken into custody, was ordered to appear before the court, and was compelled to docilely accept the judge's tirade. Unlike him, we were free to come and go as long as we observed the gallery rules. We understood, however, that we could not disrupt the hearing by expressing our disapproval of the judge's discourse. In fact, our field notes documented the many instances in which he commented on people's facial expressions in the gallery, chiding those who rolled their eyes, gasped, or sucked their teeth during his provocations, threatening to find them in contempt of court. Our collaborative ethnography revealed such orders and modes of confinement to which the people in the Milwaukee County courtrooms were differentially subjected.

We provide this insight into our work to mobilize a deeper sense of what it means to take intersectionality seriously in the context of methodology (Collins 2019). If intersectionality draws attention to the conditions of liberation that would engender our freedoms, we operationalize this lens by drawing attention to how some members of the research team were more and less free than one another and extending that to consider how the research team was more free than the adjudicants in the courthouse. By attending to the ways in which the court interpellated us all into its commitments to racial, sexual, and class hierarchy, we make visible the way that inequality is reproduced through the court's practices.

NOTES

1. We use the term "interpellation" to understand how power dominates subjects through ideologies, as evidenced in material, embodied, and physical ways (Althusser 1971). Malathi De Alwis's (1997) description of interpellation of young women in her historical ethnography on missionization practices in sixteenth-century colonial Ceylon demonstrates interpellation by looking at how colonial subjects were Christianized through embodied regimes of dress codes and sewing. Judith Butler's (1990) theory of subjectivation further expands on interpellation by identifying processes through which subject formation is imposed through intersubjective institutional, categorical, and relational interactions.

2. In a felony sexual assault court, the irony of Montana as a haven, with its own alarming rates of sexual assault, was not lost on the research team. For example, in 2015, Montana reported fifty-one rapes per one hundred thousand people, while Wisconsin reported thirty-eight per one hundred thousand people (Smith et al. 2018).

REFERENCES

Althusser, Louis, 1971. "Ideology and Ideological State Apparatuses." In *Lenin and Philosophy and Other Essays*, 85–126. New York: Verso.

Benjamin, Ruha. 2016. "Catching Our Breath: Critical Race STS and the Carceral Imagination." *Engaging Science, Technology and Society* 2:145–56.

Brown, Kenly, and Nikki Jones. 2018. "Gender, Race, and Crime: The Evolution of a Feminist Research Agenda." In *The Handbook of the Sociology of Gender*, edited by B. J. Risman, 449–57. New York: Springer.

Browne, Simone. 2015. *Dark Matters: On the Surveillance of Blackness*. Durham, NC: Duke University Press.

Butler, Judith. 1990. *Gender Trouble: Feminism and the Subversion of Identity*. New York: Routledge.

Clair, Matthew, and Amanda Woog. 2022. "Courts and the Abolition Movement." *California Law Review* 110 (1).

Collins, Patricia Hill. 2019. *Intersectionality as Critical Social Theory*. Durham, NC: Duke University Press.

Crenshaw, Kimberlé. 1991. "Mapping the Margins: Intersectionality, Identity Politics, and Violence against Women of Color." *Stanford Law Review* 43 (1): 1241–99.

De Alwis, Malathi. 1997. "The Production and Embodiment of Respectability: Gendered Demeanors in Colonial Ceylon." In *Sri Lanka: Collective Identities Revisited*, edited by Michael Roberts, 105–43. Colombo, Sri Lanka: Marga.

Flood, Dawn Rae. 2012. *Rape in Chicago: Race, Myth and the Courts*. Urbana: University of Illinois Press.

Gonzalez Van Cleve, Nicole. 2016. *Crook County: Racism and Injustice in America's Largest Criminal Court*. Stanford, CA: Stanford University Press.

Hanson, Rebecca, and Patricia Richards. 2019. *Harassed: Gender, Bodies, and Ethnographic Research*. Oakland: University of California Press.

Hlavka, Heather. 2010. "Child Sexual Abuse and Embodiment." *Sociological Studies of Children and Youth* 13:131–65.

———. 2013. "Legal Subjectivity among Youth Victims of Sexual Abuse." *Law & Social Inquiry* 39:31–61.

———. 2014. "Normalizing Sexual Violence: Young Women Account for Harassment and Abuse." *Gender & Society* 28:337–58.

———. 2017. "Speaking of Stigma and the Silence of Shame: Young Men and Sexual Victimization." *Men and Masculinities* 20 (4): 482–505.

———. 2019. "Regulating Bodies: Children and Sexual Violence." *Violence Against Women* 25 (6): 1956–79.

Hlavka, Heather, and Sameena Mulla. 2021. *Bodies in Evidence: Race, Gender, Science and Sexual Assault Adjudication*. New York: New York University Press.

Jaggar, Alison M. 1989. "Love and Knowledge: Emotion in Feminist Epistemology." *Inquiry* 32 (2): 151–76.

Kaba, Mariame. 2021. *We Do This 'til We Free Us: Abolitionist Organizing and Transforming Justice*. Chicago: Haymarket Books.

Kim, Mimi. 2018. "From Carceral Feminism to Transformative Justice: Women-of-Color Feminism and Alternatives to Incarceration." *Journal of Ethnic & Cultural Diversity in Social Work* 27 (3): 219–33.

Morgan, Rachel, and Jennifer Truman. 2020. *Criminal Victimization, 2019*. Washington, DC: US Department of Justice, Office of Justice Programs, Bureau of Justice Statistics.

Mulla, Sameena. 2014. *The Violence of Care*. New York: New York University Press.

———. 2017. "Sensing Sexual Assault: Evidencing Truth Claims in the Forensic Sensorium." In *Sensing Law*, edited by Sheryl N. Hamilton, Diana Majury, Dawn Moore, Neil Sargent, and Christiane Wilke, 195–214. New York: Routledge.

Powell, Amber Joy, Heather Hlavka, and Sameena Mulla. 2017. "Intersectionality and Credibility in Child Sexual Assault Trials." *Gender & Society* 31 (4): 457–80.

Richie, Beth E. 2012. *Arrested Justice: Black Women, Violence, and America's Prison Nation*. New York: New York University Press.

Smith, David. 1998. "An Athapaskan Way of Knowing: Chipewyan Ontology." *American Ethnologist* 25 (3): 412–32.

Smith, Sharon G., Xinjian Zhang, Kathleen C. Basile, Melissa T. Merrick, Jing Wang, Marcie-jo Kresnow, and Jieru Chen. 2018. *National Intimate Partner and Sexual Violence Survey: Data Brief—Update Release*. Atlanta: National Center for Injury Prevention and Control, Centers for Disease Control and Prevention.

Sommerville, Diane M. 2005. *Rape and Race in the Nineteenth Century South*. Chapel Hill: University of North Carolina Press.

Torres, M. Gabriela. 2019. "Feminist Anthropology Is Teamwork." *Anthropology News*, November 7, 2019.

Conclusion

Imagining: The Embrace of an Entangled, Embodied Methodological Future

APRIL D. J. PETILLO AND HEATHER R. HLAVKA

We began this volume asking readers to join us in considering some of the pressing issues with which gender violence scholars have been grappling. With the experiences collected here, we have begun a conversation about how entanglement with embodied, intersectional methodologies enhances gender violence research. This book has documented the need to reexamine how we expect to think through, research, and speak about gender violence. April D. J. Petillo came to this thinking while reckoning with advice she received to share what she considers "the spectacle" of her interlocutors' stories while maintaining their anonymity as a means to "pull people" into her research. She still regularly reckons with similar advice as junior faculty. Heather R. Hlavka recalls feeling pushed to truncate and decontextualize only those sensational bits and pieces of longer narratives of sexual violence. Both of us feel, then and now, that those were critical decision-making moments that framed the kind of gender violence researcher we aspired to be—refusing to titillate or resort to dispassionate objectivity.

What We Found

Gender violence research requires a new approach to support the new realities we share as we strive for justice in our collective lives. This conclusionary call offers what we—students, academics, and activists at the crossroads of multiple identities and entangled embodiments— have found when critically reflecting on how our identities enhance our research and thinking about why, where, and how to engage in gender violence research. Through the processes of naming, being, and witnessing, we have found that self-reflective and embodied methodologies have helped us design and conduct research that allows for

- deeper, more nuanced research engagement across varied communities;
- robust and innovative response to the ethical considerations and political challenges of feminist research;
- realistic processes for reimagining research relationships of greater equitable power balance; and
- rebuilding connections between our researcher and human selves.

What We Need

This book has also suggested some changes, particularly reimagining within the academy. The current neoliberal turn limits creative freedoms, drawing us down to its reorientation toward detached scholarship. As Wies and Haldane note in the foreword to this volume, capitalism has only offered the academy a "false promise of individual success and achievement [and] has built a world of hate and harm. This is not a world we have to continue to accept. Rethinking our methodologies allows us to remake our realities (ix)." Rather than continuing down the path, we must reorient and humanize. We must readily (re)embrace research and life that values "the primacy of identity, lived experience as knowledge, and validates the expertise that comes from the aging process and the life cycle (ix)." We need only expand our embodied imaginations and embrace our humanity (anthropological imagination) and recognize our interrelatedness (Schuller 2021). Embracing our humanity in this way also gives us insight, through the sociological imagination, into the conditions that inform choices made under duress, out of fear, or for survival. Social bonds in recognition of our interrelated lives are needed for cultural transformation, for survival, and to end gender-based violence.

Together we have argued the need to build an embodied intersectional imagination—sensitized to the processes necessary for fleshing out how our bodies reveal knowledges central to experience and truth. This building involves getting comfortable with:

- asking questions and turning inward;
- interrogating disembodied processes of knowledge-making;
- redefining the disciplinary edicts to witness and document passively; and
- recontextualizing our work by embracing our humanness—that essential, distinguishing quality of being human—and empowering each other.

The questions that began this text are only a few of the many raised when using a feminist, intersectional embodied methodology for interpersonal, gender violence research. While doing so requires turning our gaze toward ourselves, the purpose is to hold ourselves accountable to our interlocutors and to the world knowledge we cocreate. The intention is to build a more honest, equitable research relationship that engages and empowers communities in ways that are accessible, compelling, and revealing of the nuances that arise from the vigor of varied voices. Genuine entanglement with embodied methodologies is not an exercise in academic narcissism or decontextualized autobiography; instead, it is a means to appreciate how violence operates and is lived across multiple, intersecting bodies of oppressions, including our own. Therefore, we have prominently figured in this book the challenge of navigating the crossroads between researcher and interlocutor in embodied research and how to "write against the hierarchy" of these identities and positions. Revealing these entanglements here exposes the silences of hierarchies and the disciplining of bodies so that future conversations might continue to reimagine the transformative potential of embodied theory and method.

Evidence of the urgency of addressing gender violence includes a geopolitical climate that excuses white-supremacist, compulsory, settler heteropatriarchy. Simultaneously, it hypercriminalizes and incarcerates the poor, the vulnerable, and the victimized (Richie 2012) though it remains mainly blind to colonialism and able-bodyism. Conversations about safety, justice, and recourse from gendered violence have increased, but that is not enough. People invested in the status quo are still not held accountable. Narrow definitions of gender violence obfuscate state practices and policies, and compulsory aggression and control are continually interwoven into our social systems (Richie 2012; Roberts 1999). Thus, our work is vital to the safety, solidarity, support, and liberation of our and our interlocutors' personhood. It is necessary if we are serious about our reciprocal relationships and committed to mutual environments of learning and unlearning.

Even as we have discussed the need for humanness in our work, academic systems continue to encourage dispassionate engagement, framing our humanity as an unwelcome, unreliable research practice. Proof of that is evident in our training. While becoming researchers, we are encouraged to leave our ordinary humanness behind, treat it as a weakness to overcome, or hide it under layers of sleepless nights spent wondering, "Do I belong here? What is the value of my work if objectivity is not my goal?" (see Harding 1987). But this reach for in/unhuman objectivity is unbearable. Frontline workers have long understood that the most accurate prevalence rate of gender violence is the best empirical study's numbers multiplied by three. This adage rests on the idea that at least one-third of victim/survivors will not discuss their experiences because of a sense of shame supported by supremacist rape culture. Another one-third will not discuss their experience because of cultural suspicion cast on them on the basis of their identities. Fealty to objectivity has not delivered on its promises.

With such untenable options, operating as an "unsettled witness" (Fukushima 2016) reframes the disciplinary goal of witnessing lived realities. Doing so not only requires us to break norms and purposefully redirect action in the research environment but also refuses the settler innocence that the academy encourages us to claim (Tuck and Yang 2012). It allows us to be fully attentive to the broad spectrum of power dynamics operating across multiple identities (Garba and Sorentino 2020). The refusal to "settle in" to the violences we are privy to as researchers also positions us better to meet interlocutor expectations (Davis 2013), aptly demonstrated through the experiences shared in this collection. This unsettling presents an opportunity to reject reductive, dehumanizing training concerning interlocutors' and our own experiences of systemic injustice. Unsettled witnessing then necessarily informs documentation, encouraging different methods of writing about interlocutor experience (see the chapters of Tynes, Schwarz, and Powell, Mulla, and Hlavka in this volume), autoethnographic texts (see the chapters of Tynes, Moore and Hofeller, Mokhtar, and Small in this volume), and otherwise representing lived realities (see the chapters of Brigden, Bloom, and Whittaker in this volume). Through the naming, being, and unsettled witnessing demonstrated in these contributors' accounts, interlocutors' and researchers' complex lives and responses are amplified as a powerful antidote to their misrepresentation or erasure. They call into question the usual means of flattening experiences through normative research processes.

What We Recommend

Our recommendations sound deceptively simple. As detailed in chapter 1 and the introductions for each of the three parts, we believe that applying entangled, embodied methodology in gender violence research requires collaborative effort. It requires team-based research collaborations, listening through discomfort, unsettled witnessing, and an embodied reimagination that can empower each other for social justice and change. It also requires humanizing through a faithful mirror to lovingly, playfully reflect the ways we do and can engage world-making together (Lugones 1987). We can be creative and open. "We are not self-important, we are not fixed in particular constructions of ourselves, which is part of saying that we are open to self-construction" (Lugones 1987, 16). María Lugones positions feminist coalitions rooted in the textures of differences and the ability to see how locating oneself in the world enables one to see how the parts fit together (Lugones and Spelman 1983). Lugones goes on to say, "The reason why I think that travelling to someone's 'world' is a way of identifying with them is because by travelling to their 'world' we can understand *what it is to be them and what it is to be ourselves in their eyes.* Only when we have travelled to each other's 'worlds' are we fully subjects to each other" (1987, 17). This all hinges on our willingness to make the researcher visible in the process—from method to interpretation to analysis—and to push back against dominant narratives and canons that have been historically produced by economically and racially privileged men (Sprague 2005). We must understand that we are all implicated in violence when we are grounded or complicit "in the same systems we are committed to opposing" (Russo 2018, 33). We must change our gender violence research processes to see colonialism and able-bodyism, to reconsider carceral regimes, not only to make space but to hold space for people of color, queer and transgender people, immigrants, and gender-nonconforming folks in our work, our institutions, and our lives. We must hold each other accountable so that doing the work and teaching our students look, feel, and operate as "world traveling" (Lugones 1987) and "world-making." Humanizing all ourselves / our selves is a life-or-death proposition because gender violence research and work can, indeed, be life or death for all of us.

We gathered and refined this text, and this conclusion, at a time when we all need collective hope and a vision to continue the good work of feminist research. Our worlds are becoming increasingly fragmented, surveilled, and hyperreliant on algorithmic displays of disembodied realities. Coupled with extremism, attacks against facts and truth, we are becoming more detached from reality as a culture, even as many communities are pulling each other inward (Kaba 2021). We take seriously our calling as researchers to serve as critical public intellectuals—not as an elite focused on advancement in academic careers but instead as a human resource participating in conversations about the public interest, responding to the social and cultural problems that impact all of society. It is our job to question, think, reflect, offer insight, and critique. Though many people might expect that our role is to remain impartial at all costs, we assert that a dispassionate position concerning equity, safety, and protection—all essential concepts in gender violence work—maintained from behind the shield of our disciplines serves no one. A response to the times in which we find ourselves doing this work requires a willingness to address related global issues, and our futures require us to expand our sociological and anthropological imaginations.

In unprecedented times of cultural disruption, social and economic precarity, racial injustices, and the deleterious impact of COVID-19 on our communities, our critical work is, perhaps paradoxically, especially necessary. In such times, we may find ourselves haunted and tormented by the unease of a sociality (Gordon 2008) that requires us to ignore the ordinary humanness encouraging us to name our corporeal realities, recognize and respond from our shared being, and unsettle our witnessing. But suppressing that in favor of reactionary calls for unmeasured "cohesion," unexamined "unity," and "common purposes" that require sacrifices borne by a specific few does not adequately respond to our global needs. Thus, we are called to build life-affirming institutions and movements generated from the ground up. The nature of the times we are in invites us to develop our personal and collective capacity to respond to harm and build supportive communities. This gender violence work is buoyed by approaching embodied methodology firmly grounded in the intersectional realities for individuals, communities, and researchers while recognizing that these three positions are hardly ever discrete. It is time to roll up our sleeves, take a deep breath, and dive back into the work with a new, profoundly entangled, embodied focus as we "world" travel (Lugones 1987) and pull each other inward (Kaba 2021).

REFERENCES

Davis, Dána-Ain. 2013. "Border Crossings: Intimacy and Feminist Activist Ethnography in the Age of Neoliberalism." In *Feminist Activist Ethnography: Counterpoints to Neoliberalism in North America*, edited by Christa Craven and Dána-Ain Davis, 23–38. Lanham, MD: Lexington Books.

Fukushima, Annie Isabel. 2016. "An American Haunting: Unsettling Witnessing in Transnational Migration, the Ghost Case, and Human Trafficking." *Feminist Formations* 28 (1): 146–65.

Garba, Tapji, and Sara-Maria Sorentino. 2020. "Slavery Is a Metaphor: A Critical Commentary on Eve Tuck and K. Wayne Yang's 'Decolonization Is Not a Metaphor.'" *Antipode* 52 (3): 764–82.

Gordon, Avery. 2008. *Ghostly Matters Haunting and the Sociological Imagination*. 2nd ed. Minneapolis: University of Minnesota Press.

Harding, Sandra. 1987. "The Method Question." *Hypatia* 2 (3): 19–35. https://doi.org/10.1111/j.1527-2001.1987.tb01339.x.

Kaba, Mariame. 2021. *We Do This 'til We Free Us: Abolitionist Organizing and Transforming Justice*. Chicago: Haymarket Books.

Lugones, María. 1987. "Playfulness, 'World'-Travelling, and Loving Perception." *Hypatia* 2 (2): 3–19. https://doi.org/10.1111/j.1527-2001.1987.tb01062.x.

Lugones, Maria, and Elizabeth V. Spelman. 1983. "Have We Got a Theory For You! Feminist Theory, Cultural Imperialism and the Demand for 'the Woman's Voice.'" *Women's Studies International Forum* 6 (6): 573–81.

Richie, Beth E. 2012. *Arrested Justice: Black Women, Violence, and America's Prison Nation*. New York: New York University Press.

Roberts, Dorothy E. 1999. *Killing the Black Body: Race, Reproduction, and the Meaning of Liberty*. New York: Vintage.

Russo, Ann. 2018. *Feminist Accountability: Disrupting Violence and Transforming Power*. New York: New York University Press.

Schuller, Mark. 2021. *Humanity's Last Stand: Confronting Global Catastrophe.* New Brunswick, NJ: Rutgers University Press.

Sprague, Joey. 2005. *Feminist Methodologies for Critical Researchers: Bridging Differences.* Lanham, MD: Rowman and Littlefield.

Tuck, Eve, and K. Wayne Yang. 2012. "Decolonization Is Not a Metaphor." *Decolonization: Indigeneity, Education & Society* 1 (1): 1–40.

ACKNOWLEDGMENTS

This collection is the product of many people in both big and small ways.

We are grateful for those who survive gender violence. Whether that harm has been acknowledged or not, this collection is part of our effort to create a better, safer, and more just world without this violence. We believe that is possible. We believe that our job as researchers is to illuminate the conditions that create an environment where this violence continues. We believe that the academy is accountable for contributing to those harms. If you have shared your experience with us, thank you for your trust. If not, thank you for knowing and maintaining your boundaries. This work is possible because of both.

We thank, of course, the scholars who entrusted their brilliance, creativity, passion, and time to this project. The act of reflection is embodied work, and it is not easy. Addressing gender violence requires multiple methods and approaches because these issues do not originate from one source, either. We are thrilled to think through the possibilities with you, and you always inspire us.

This work began as conversations across several conferences, including those of the Association for Feminist Anthropology (the American Anthropological Association), the Law and Society Association, the National Women's Studies Association, and the American Studies Association. Additionally, the Society for Applied Anthropology's Gender-Based Violence Thematic Interest Group (GBV-TIG) has been our home. This group, initiated by Jennifer R. Wies and Hillary J. Haldane, has supported good/right work and amplified its members' innovative thought at every step. Without the leadership and encouragement provided by Jennifer, Hillary, and now Elizabeth Wirtz and Allison Bloom, the discussions so vital to this end product could not have happened.

We are particularly grateful to Sameena Mulla, who ignited conversations and brought us together as coeditors. Your gentle but firm nudges feel more powerful than they may appear. You are tenacious in the best of ways and not to be underestimated. Thank you for investing those gifts in this work with faith in our ability to see it through.

We are also particularly grateful to Jennifer Hammer, New York University Press, and peer readers for embracing an edited collection pitched midpandemic with vigor and verve. Your suggestions, requests, and questions undoubtedly made for a better version of this text and a better process for addressing these issues with studied insight grounded in the complicated lives and realities of surviving gender violence, researching, and writing about it.

We also want to thank the Institute for Women's Leadership (IWL) at Marquette University and the College of Social and Behavioral Sciences at Northern Arizona University for fiscally supporting the final stages of indexing this work.

April would like to thank Heather for sharing her knowledge, expertise, and experience along this coediting journey. It has been more enjoyable to do this with someone who knows their boundaries, says it straight, and can hang with the kooky randomness even as deadlines approach. I could not have asked for a better, more hilarious partner on this journey. Shireen Roshanravan, you have proven yourself to be more than a work colleague. Despite laughing at the suggestion that you might be a good mentor, your willingness to listen, share, and support with honesty, integrity, and kindness are some of your secret weapons. I am honored to witness these fierce skills. Thank you for sharing them with me. Michael and Sofia, the best husband and pup that anyone could wish for—thank you. Despite long nights, endless meetings, delayed walks, and insane coffee requests, you gifted me your patience and presence. You remind me why I think this work is important and always help me see a better, truer version of myself. Thank you.

Heather is deeply grateful to April for her vision, her patience, humor, and wisdom. Our coediting has been a collective process of strength, compassion, and devotion to the work, to our contributors and their voices, and to survival in all its many forms. It is wonderful to share the entanglements of our worlds together with deep appreciation and dedication to feminist friendships. How else would this be possible? Heather is also grateful to Kevin and James, my partners always, for making every day a new and exciting journey. Thank you for grounding me, settling me, and feeding me.

ABOUT THE EDITORS

APRIL D. J. PETILLO is Assistant Professor of Public Sociology in the Department of Sociology at Northern Arizona University.

HEATHER R. HLAVKA is Associate Professor of Criminology and Law Studies in the Department of Social and Cultural Sciences at Marquette University. Her interdisciplinary work focuses on sexual violence, gender and intersectionality, trauma, sociolegal studies, and feminist methods, and she is the author (with Sameena Mulla) of *Bodies in Evidence: Race, Gender, and Science in Sexual Assault Adjudication.*

ABOUT THE CONTRIBUTORS

ALLISON BLOOM is Assistant Professor of Anthropology in the Sociology and Anthropology Department at Moravian University in Bethlehem, Pennsylvania. Her research interests include medical and applied anthropology, gender studies, immigration, Latino/a studies, and health and social services inequities.

NOELLE BRIGDEN is Associate Professor of International Relations in the Department of Political Science at Marquette University. She is the author of *The Migrant Passage: Clandestine Journeys from Central America*.

HILLARY J. HALDANE is Professor of Anthropology and Director of General Education at Quinnipiac University. Her research focuses on the expertise of frontline workers in Aotearoa and Australia.

STEPHANIE HOFELLER is a writer, artist, activist, and Gonzo journalist who has recently found a calling as a survivor advocate, researching and writing about gender-based violence and the violence inherent in all hierarchical systems. Find more of her work at https://shutupstephanie.org.

HASNAA MOKHTAR is Postdoctoral Associate at Rutgers University's Center for Women's Global Leadership. She is a scholar, researcher, and activist with expertise on the Arabian Gulf, focusing on narratives of Muslim survivors of gender-based violence. Her doctoral research focused on narrative power and the invisible trauma of gendered violence in Kuwait.

DAWN MOORE is a queer settler and Professor of Law and Legal Studies at Carleton University. Moore researches interpersonal and gender-based violence, prisoners' rights, prison abolition, substance use, and Canada's ongoing genocide of Indigenous peoples.

SAMEENA MULLA is Associate Professor in the Department of Women's, Gender, and Sexuality Studies at Emory University in Atlanta, Georgia. She is the author of *The Violence of Care: Rape Victims, Forensic Nurses, and Sexual Assault Intervention* and, with Heather R. Hlavka, *Bodies in Evidence: Race, Gender, and Science in Sexual Assault Adjudication*.

AMBER JOY POWELL is Assistant Professor in the Department of Sociology & Criminology at the University of Iowa and a former American Bar Foundation and National Science Foundation Fellow. Her work examines the intersections of law, violence, race, gender, and sexuality.

CORINNE SCHWARZ is Assistant Professor of Gender, Women's, and Sexuality Studies (GWST) at Oklahoma State University. Her research interests include sociolegal approaches to gender, violence, and frontline work.

JAMIE L. SMALL is Associate Professor of Sociology at the University of Dayton. She studies the intersection of law, crime, and gender. In 2020–22, she was an AAAS Science & Technology Policy Fellow, placed at the US Agency for International Development as a Gender-Based Violence Advisor.

BRENDANE TYNES (she/her) is an interpersonal violence survivor, queer Black feminist theorist, and writer from Columbia, South Carolina. She is an Anthropology PhD Candidate at Columbia University and a cohost of *Zora's Daughters Podcast*, a Black feminist anthropological intervention on popular culture.

CATHERINE WHITTAKER is Assistant Professor of Social and Cultural Anthropology at the Goethe University Frankfurt/Main (Germany) and a visiting scholar at the University of California San Diego (2020–22). Her research specializes on structures of violence, gender, and Indigeneity in Mexico and the US-Mexican borderlands.

JENNIFER R. WIES is Professor of Anthropology and Associate Provost at Eastern Kentucky University, a regional, public school of opportunity in Appalachia. She is an applied anthropologist dedicated to teaching and practicing anthropology, with research focusing on violence intervention and response systems in the United States, including domestic shelters, campus sexual violence programs, and most recently, opioid misuse treatment programs.

INDEX

able-bodied, 107, 110; able-bodyism, 177, 179. *See also* disability
abolition, 169. *See also* anticarceral feminism
Abu-Lughod, Lila, 112, 113, 114
accountability, 3, 11, 34, 107, 117, 168–171, 177, 180
Adelman, Madelaine, 83, 87
advocates, 3, 15; equality and, 67; political solidarity with, 80–85, 88–90; terminology and, 40n2; violence and exploitation by, 62, 68. *See also* frontline workers
affective experiences: researchers' entanglements, 2, 6, 22–23, 43–45, 53–55, 76, 101, 164–166, 170–171; and "speaking for others," 96–97. *See also* emotions
agency, 6, 11, 39, 117; healing and, 155; silence as, 47; state violence and, 58–59
Agustín, Laura, 94
Ahmad, Attiya, 16
Ahmed, Sara, 19, 52, 57, 94
Al-Ali, Nadje, 107, 110, 117, 118
Alcoff, Linda, 94, 96
Algar, Hamid, 114
Allaghi, Farida, 116
Almana, Aisha, 116
Al-Sayegh, Fatma, 111
Al-Shammaa, Khalid, 112
AlShehabi, Omar H., 108, 111
Althusser, Louis, 172n1
Altunışık, Meliha Benli, 108
Ángel, Miguel, 44
Angelou, Maya, 40

anger, vii, 11, 94, 100–102, 137, 151
anthropological imagination, 20, 176, 180
anticarceral feminism, 93, 161, 169, 179
anti-trafficking narratives, 76–77, 92–103
Anzaldúa, Gloria, 18, 19
Arab Gulf countries, 77, 106–118
Arat-Koç, Sedef, 113
athleticism, 146–147, 149, 151, 153–156
attorneys, 127, 130–142
audiences, 10, 86, 88–89, 139
autoethnography, 123, 130–142
autonomy, 3, 134, 138, 141, 154–155
Aztecs, 44, 48

Battle, Nishaun T., 30
beauty norms, 147–148, 150, 153
Beblawi, Hazem, 108
being (reflective entanglements), 5, 73–77, 124, 176
Benjamin, Ruha, 160
Bennett, Lerone, 106
Bernstein, Elizabeth, 103
Bethea, Charles, 70
Betts, Connor, 142
Bilge, Sirma, 21
binaries, 18, 21, 101
biographies, 13, 133, 136, 177
BIPoC (Black, Indigenous, and/or people of color) communities, 73, 77; sexual assault adjudication and, 128, 159–172. *See also* Arab Gulf countries; Black feminist ethnography; Black men; Black women; Indigenous women; Latina women; racism and racial injustices